THE SARBANES-OXLEY ACT: AN INTRODUCTION

The Sarbanes-Oxley Act
An Introduction

Sanjay Anand

Colophon

Title:	The Sarbanes-Oxley Act: An Introduction
Author:	Sanjay Anand
Editor:	Jayne Wilkinson
Publisher:	Van Haren Publishing, Zaltbommel. www.vanharen.net
Design and layout:	CO2 Premedia BV, Amersfoort, NL
ISBN:	978 908753 083 9
Edition:	First edition, first impression, July 2008

© SOX Institute.org

All rights reserved. No part of this publication may be reproduced in any form by print, photo print, microfilm or by any other means, without the written permission of the publisher. Although this publication has been composed with much care, neither author, nor editor, nor publisher can accept liability for damage caused by possible errors and/or incompleteness in this publication.
The publisher will endeavour to correct any errors in subsequent editions when they are notified.

ITIL® is a Registered Trade Mark, and a Registered Community Trade Mark of the Office of Government Commerce, and is Registered in the US Patent and Trademark Office.
CoBiT® is a registered trademark of the Information Systems Audit and Control Association (ISACA)/IT Governance Institute (ITGI). SOXBoK and SOX Institute are registered trademarks of Sarbanes Oxley Group llc, New Jersey.

Contents

INTRODUCTION: XI
An Introduction to the Sarbanes-Oxley Body of Knowledge (SOXBoK)
from the SOX Institute

CHAPTER 1: 1
Public Company Accounting Oversight Board

CHAPTER 2: 43
Auditor Independence

CHAPTER 3: 59
Corporate Responsibility

CHAPTER 4: 89
Enhanced Financial Disclosures

CHAPTER 5: 131
Analyst Conflict of Interest

CHAPTER 6: 137
Commission Resources and Authority

CHAPTER 7: 145
Studies and Reports

CHAPTER 8: 161
Corporate and Criminal Fraud Accountability

CHAPTER 9: 175
White-Collar Crime Penalty Enhancements

CHAPTER 10: 183
Corporate Tax Returns

CHAPTER 11: 185
Corporate Fraud Accountability

References 195
Glossary 197
Abbreviations 209

Appendix A 211
Appendix B 215
Appendix C 219
Appendix D 221
Appendix E 225

Credits in Alphabetical Sequence

Full Name SOXBoK Team Member	Credentials	Job Title	Company	Location	Knowledge Team
Czarniewy, Kim			EP Medical Systems	West Berlin, NJ	F&A
De Marco, Josie	PMP	Director	Project Management Office, USA	San Carlos, CA	IT
Fellenz, Beth Anne		Senior Auditor		Novi, MI	I&E Audit
Gbenle, Isaac Toyin	MBA, CSOX-IT	Technical Compliance	ESPN, Inc.	Meriden, CT	L&C
Glynn, Kathy	CPA	Partner	Gap Resources, LLP SOX Compliance Consulting	Glenview, IL	I&E Audit Team Lead
LaCagnina, John	CSOX, CISA, PMP, CobiT certified, MCSE, MCP+I, CNA	IT Auditor/ Security and Compliance Analyst		West Milford, NJ	SOXBoK Board
Ledlow, Johna	PMP, CSOXP	Project Manager		Trussville, AL	IT
Noel, Debra		Project and Process Manager	EDS	Rochester Hills, MI	F&A
O'Keeffe, Jim	PMP, CISM, CDP	Consulting Manager	Sycor Americas	Gibsonia, PA	Project Leader
Owen, Richard Mays	PMP, PhD		Richard Owen International (ROI)	Houston, TX	L&C Team Lead
Schwind, Robert	MBA, CSOXP, CISA	President	GKBN Technologies, Inc	Albany, NY	SOXBoK Board
South, Cindy	PMP	Sr. Project Manager	Yellow Book USA	Malvern, PA	D&W
Turner, Heather	CAPM	Project Governance Specialist	Olympic Health Management Systems	Sedro Woolley, WA	D&W

Full Name	Credentials	Job Title	Company	Location
Research Credits:				
Czarniewy, Kim			EP Medical Systems	West Berlin, NJ
De Marco, Josie	PMP	Director	Project Management Office, USA	San Carlos, CA
Fellenz, Beth Anne		Senior Auditor		Novi, MI
Gbenle, Isaac Toyin	MBA, CSOX-IT	Technical Compliance	ESPN, Inc.	Meriden, CT
Glynn, Kathy	CPA	Partner	Gap Resources, LLP SOX Compliance Consulting	Glenview, IL
Ledlow, Johna	PMP, CSOXP	Project Manager		Trussville, AL
Noel, Debra		Project and Process Manager	EDS	Rochester Hills, MI
O'Keeffe, Jim	PMP, CISM, CDP	Consulting Manager	Sycor Americas	Gibsonia, PA
Owen, Richard Mays	PMP, PhD		Richard Owen International (ROI)	Houston, TX
Schwind, Robert	MBA, CSOXP, CISA	President	GKBN Technologies, Inc	Albany, NY
South, Cindy	PMP	Sr. Project Manager	Yellow Book USA	Malvern, PA
Turner, Heather	CAPM	Project Governance Specialist	Olympic Health Management Systems	Sedro Woolley, WA
Writing Credits:				
De Marco, Josie	PMP	Director	Project Management Office, USA	San Carlos, CA
Fellenz, Beth Anne		Senior Auditor		Novi, MI
Ledlow, Johna	PMP, CSOXP	Project Manager		Trussville, AL
O'Keeffe, Jim	PMP, CISM, CDP	Consulting Manager	Sycor Americas	Gibsonia, PA
Owen, Richard Mays	PMP, PhD		Richard Owen International (ROI)	Houston, TX
Schwind, Robert	MBA, CSOXP, CISA	President	GKBN Technologies, Inc	Albany, NY
South, Cindy	PMP	Sr. Project Manager	Yellow Book USA	Malvern, PA
Turner, Heather	CAPM	Project Governance Specialist	Olympic Health Management Systems	Sedro Woolley, WA

Full Name	Credentials	Job Title	Company	Location
Editing Credits:				
De Marco, Josie	PMP	Director	Project Management Office, USA	San Carlos, CA
Fellenz, Beth Anne		Senior Auditor		Novi, MI
Ledlow, Johna	PMP, CSOXP	Project Manager		Trussville, AL
O'Keeffe, Jim	PMP, CISM, CDP	Consulting Manager	Sycor Americas	Gibsonia, PA
Owen, Richard Mays	PMP, PhD		Richard Owen International (ROI)	Houston, TX
Schwind, Robert	MBA, CSOXP, CISA	President	GKBN Technologies, Inc	Albany, NY
South, Cindy	PMP	Sr. Project Manager	Yellow Book USA	Malvern, PA
Turner, Heather	CAPM	Project Governance Specialist	Olympic Health Management Systems	Sedro Woolley, WA
Reviewer Credits:				
Carrizo, Ana María Rita	Public Accountant, CIA, CISA	Specialist Auditor	Deloitte & Co, member of Deloitte Touche	Buenos Aires, Argentina
Cesareo, Carol S.	CSOXP, CIA Candidate	Associate Director, Financial Compliance	PharmaNet	Princeton, NJ
Comstock, Norman L. Jr	CIA, CISA, CISSP, CSOXP, CCSA	Managing Director	UHY Advisors	Houston, TX
Hall, Rena L.	CSOXP, CICS	VP, Audit - SOX Project Manager	Midwest Banc Holdings, Inc.	Melrose Park, IL
Kromberg, Norman	CISA, National Bank Examiner, CQA	Chief Operating Officer	Before It's Time Inc.	Omaha, NE
Leidecker, Jack D.	CISA, CISSP, CISM, CBM, CSOXP, NSA-IAM, NSA-IEM	President	GRMCC.com	San Jose, Ca
Leipold, Kent	M.B.A., C.B.M.	Auditor IV	Texas Department of Transportation	Austin, Texas
Peterson, Alice				
R, Kohila	ACA, CFA, MBA	Consultant	Atlantis Management Services	Chennai, India
Wynne, Brenda	CSOXP	Information Specialist	Alcon Laboratories	Fort Worth, TX

INTRODUCTION:

An Introduction to the Sarbanes-Oxley Body of Knowledge (SOXBoK) from the SOX Institute

'By practitioners for practitioners'

The *Sarbanes-Oxley Body of Knowledge* (SOXBoK) has been developed by a select group of volunteers and recruits from the growing, active membership of the SOX Institute. Every member of the team is an active practitioner in at least one area of Sarbanes-Oxley compliance efforts within public companies. The SOXBoK was completed in three, distinct phases:

- Phase I of the project, involved forming several small teams to complete initial scope planning, research and content development, driven by team leads with expertise in specific Knowledge Areas to include:
    - Finance and Accounting
    - Information Technology
    - Legal and Ethical Compliance
    - Internal and External Audit
- Phase II of the project, involved a single, smaller team with cross-functional representation focused on knowledge sharing and analysis of the content, focusing on fact checking the content submitted by the Phase I activities.
- Phase III of the project, involved the same team as Phase II, with members now working directly with the SOX Institute Board of Directors to fine-tune the content, obtain and incorporate public commentary, and co-ordinate with the publisher to edit the book into its final format.

The Sarbanes-Oxley Act of 2002 (SOA or SOX Act) had far-reaching implications for the operations of public companies, which were greater than any other legislation to date. Large publicly traded companies are required by law to comply with the guidelines of the SOX Act; however, more and more mid-size and non-public companies are making the choice to comply with the SOX Act to instill greater stakeholder confidence in their operations and financials.

The Sarbanes-Oxley Act: An Introduction strives to align itself with the SOX Institute's objectives: The SOX Institute was created to enable individuals and enterprises to:
- freely share and exchange SOX-related information, expertise and experiences
- enable members to understand and appreciate the implications of SOX on their industry, their companies, their careers and their jobs
- Encourage the industry-wide standards of SOX competence
- take SOX compliance to a whole new level, both in the US, and around the world

The SOX Institute (now known as the Governance, Risk, Compliance (GRC) Institute) has, since its inception in 2003, organized over 100 training sessions, published four books on the Sarbanes-Oxley (SOX) Act, and trained more than 2,000 professionals and executives in SOX Act compliance, across the US, Canada, Europe, the Indian sub-continent and Asia.

The SOXBoK is intended to be a reference document for practitioners who are responsible for implementing the Sarbanes–Oxley Act of 2002 ('SOX') within their organizations. The content of the guide is written in a clear style appropriate for any level, from absolute beginners to those who want to become professionals in their audit-related fields. The SOXBoK has been developed by industry practitioners to:
- establish a consensus mechanism for delineating the knowledge and skills required to be a professional
- characterize standard practices of the profession
- guide the development of quality knowledge and skill competency assessment
- provide a background for curriculum development efforts throughout academia

The SOXBok includes each title and section of the SOX Act in its entirety. All 11 Titles and 66 sections of the SOA of 2002 were analyzed and documented in the SOXBoK. Each Title and section of the SOX Act is summarized and categorized for easy reference and comprehension, and industry best practices are discussed from the practitioner's perspective.

While developing and finalizing this Introduction, the team considered the following content and editorial assertions:
- **Completeness** – all elements in the SOX Act are addressed
- **Accuracy** – the right level of detail and instruction
- **Actionable** – how would you implement this section?
- **Single Source** – direct references within the SOX Act (eg Securities Exchange Act of 1934) are explained within the synopsis
- **Consistency** – flow, style, presentation
- **Clarity** – fully explained, clear, concise, readable
- **Relevance** – relevant to the section discussed and relevant to the audience

SOX-Specific Terminology and Abbreviations

This Introduction uses terminology that is particular to the audit, legal or accounting professions. Terms and acronyms that are consistently used throughout this publication are defined below. Additional terminology is defined in the Glossary:
- **GASP** – Generally Accepted SOX Principle is a practice that is the best response to a given section of the SOX Act
- **Issuer** – public company, which must issue financial reports according to Securities and Exchange Commission (SEC) regulations and/or the SOX Act
- **PCAOB** – Public Company Accounting Oversight Board
- **SEC** – Securities and Exchange Commission
- **SOX** – Interpretation of the Sarbanes-Oxley Act of 2002
- **Audit Partner** – accountant with primary responsibility for attesting to the adequacy of the issuer's compliance with the regulations in the SOA

SOX Processes

This section identifies key processes, domains, and Knowledge Areas associated with each SOX Title. SOX processes are the steps needed to comply with SOX requirements within multiple business functions, impacted by each section within identified domains, including:

- **Regulations for Others** – SOX requirements that apply to government agencies, independent accounting firms, or other groups that are not part of the issuing company; detailed knowledge of these regulations is not integral to Issuer complian ce with the SOX Act, but practitioners should be aware of these sections and Titles to build their awareness of the whole process
- **Planning** – setting up committees, preliminary preparation work, building the underlying structure for adequately responding to SOX requirements
- **Risk Analysis** – identifying where the financial risks lie, which ultimately determines which process controls will need to be evaluated and attested to by executive management
- **Control Assessment** – identifying which controls/processes are in place and determining whether they address the financial risks
- **Control Testing** – systematically selecting samples from each control/process, and evaluating whether the process and practice is effective
- **Co-ordinating with Auditors** – co-ordinating with internal audit resources to plan, assess and report on internal controls; working effectively with external audit to expedite independent testing and evaluation of management's testing
- **Control Deficiencies and Remediation** – once a control has been deemed ineffective, this process identifies the root cause(s) of the deficiency and how to fix it; then re-testing of controls is performed to clear associated audit comments
- **Reporting and Communication** – specifies which reports are required, what formats should be used, how frequently reports should be prepared and submitted, and by whom
- **Evaluation and Control Enhancement** – determining which effective controls/processes are not operating as well as they could be, and then making improvements

- **Sustaining** – building effective controls/processes into your company's daily routine for strong, reliable reporting capabilities
- **Audit Compliance and Enforcement** – what to do if serious material findings result in a Federal investigation or court case

SOX Domains

Domains, within the context of SOX compliance, are disciplinary overlays that aid in the understanding and implementation of the intent of the SOX Act. The objective is to ensure that auditors remain *independent*; corporations and auditors are *accountable* to the public for the numbers they publish; an independent body *governs* financial reporting processes; sufficient measures are in place to *deter* fraudulent activity; financial activities are *transparent* enough to allow fraud detection to occur; and if fraud is detected, somebody is held *responsible* for it. Domains help answer the question, 'what gets accomplished or achieved as a result of this section of the SOX Act?'

Summary of Domains by Section
Indexed By Topic

Independence: an environment where auditing bodies are not affiliated with or controlled by an issuer, and therefore are more likely to issue an objective opinion

Section	Description
Section 103	Independence standards and rules
Section 104	PCAOB periodically inspects and assesses registered public accounting firm work
Section 201	Registered public accounting firms prohibited from performing both auditing and other services that may present a conflict of interest
Section 202	Audit committee, independent from the company, approves and oversees all registered public accounting firm work
Section 203	Lead audit partner and reviewing partner's primary responsibility for an issuer's audit limited to 5 years
Section 204	All registered public accounting firms must submit regular reports to the company's audit committee
Section 205	Audit committee comprised of members of Board of Directors
Section 206	Limitations on former registered accounting firm or its employee acting as director/officer for issuer
Section 301	Audit committee independence

Accountability: answering to a higher level or regulating body	
Section 102	Public accounting firms must register with, and pay annual fees to, PCAOB
Section 302	Management responsibility for design, implementation, evaluation and reporting of disclosure controls to SEC
Section 401	SEC requirements for filing financial statements
Section 403	Stock transactions must be filed with SEC
Section 404	Issuer must report weaknesses of Internal Control Over Financial Reporting to registered public accounting firm; registered public accounting firm must attest to, and report on, assessment of internal controls made by management to SEC
Section 405	Exemptions from requirements of Sections 401, 402 and 404
Section 406	Failure to adopt a 'code of ethics' must be disclosed to SEC
Section 407	Issuers must include a financial expert in their audit committee
Section 501	Registered securities association or national securities exchange must modify their rules relating to securities analysts findings
Section 906	Directors/officers must certify every periodic report submitted to the SEC, or else face criminal penalties
Section 1001	CEO is individually accountable and responsible for financial reporting results
Section 1103	During cease-and-desist proceeding, SEC can issue temporary order requiring the issuer to escrow extraordinary payments
Section 1104	US Sentencing Commission must review and update sentencing guidelines applicable to securities and accounting fraud and related offences
Governance: the continuous exercise of authority over and the performance of functions for a political unit	
Section 101	PCAOB governance of internal and external auditors
Section 103	PCAOB establishes rules and requirements for auditing
Section 106	PCAOB oversees foreign accounting firms
Section 107	SEC oversees the PCAOB operations
Section 108	Accounting standards acceptable to SEC
Section 109	PCAOB funding and budgeting guidelines
Section 202	Audit committee pre-approval required for all registered public accounting firm activities
Section 203	SEC requires a mandatory auditor rotation
Section 204	All registered public accounting firms must disclose key company financial information to the audit committee
Section 205	Audit committee oversees registered public accounting firm
Section 206	SEC limits who can act as director/officer for issuer
Section 207	US Comptroller General to publish a study on mandatory auditor rotation effectiveness
Section 208	Registered public accounting firm cannot perform audit activities if engaged in activities prohibited by Securities Exchange Act of 1934
Section 209	Applicability of Title II requirements determined by appropriate state authorities
Section 307	Escalation process for attorneys reporting deficiencies

Section 404	Issuer must report weaknesses of internal control over financial reporting to registered public accounting firm; registered public accounting firm must attest to, and report on, assessment of internal controls made by management to SEC
Section 408	SEC right to review financial statements and disclosures at will
Section 601	Additional funds appropriated to SEC
Section 602	SEC authority to reject or refuse any auditor
Section 603	Prohibition of brokers, dealers, and issuers from participating in penny stock transactions
Section 604	SEC authority to censure or restrict an associated person or a broker or dealer from engaging in the business of securities, banking or insurance
Section 701	US General Accounting Office (GOA) must submit a study concerning 'Public Accounting Firms-Mandated Study on Consolidation and Competition'
Section 702	SEC must submit a report addressing each of the topics identified for Commission study in the Sarbanes-Oxley Act
Section 703	SEC must submit a report and study addressing violations by security professionals
Section 704	SEC must submit a study on enforcement actions
Section 705	Analysis by the US General Accounting Office on role of Investment Banks with respect to the corporate scandals conducted by Enron and WorldCom executives
Section 802	Criminal penalties for altering documents in the course of an investigation
Section 804	Statute of limitation for filing a fraud claim
Section 805	US Sentencing Commission to revisit and update the sentences relating to obstruction of justice and extensive criminal fraud
Section 807	Criminal penalties for defrauding shareholders of publicly traded companies
Section 1104	US Sentencing Commission must review and update sentencing guidelines applicable to securities and accounting fraud and related offenses
Deterrence: the measurements taken to prevent in appropriate behavior using fear, especially of punishment	
Section 102	Unlawful for an unregistered public accounting firm to issue audit report
Section 104	PCAOB periodically inspects and assesses registered public accounting firm work
Section 105	Disciplinary action against registered public accounting firms for non-compliance with investigatory proceedings
Section 107	SEC has the authority to remove PCAOB board members who have willfully violated the SOX Act
Section 108	Establishing accounting standards
Section 303	Employees, officers, etc. are prohibited from influencing the outcome of an audit
Section 304	If restatement filed for 'material non-compliance', directors/officers must reimburse issuer for certain types of compensation
Section 305	SEC has authority to prohibit an individual from serving as a director/officer
Section 308	Civil penalties and repayment to investors may be required when violations of the federal securities acts occur involving fraud

Section 802	Criminal penalties for altering documents in the course of an investigation
Section 902	Increased penalties for criminal fraud offenses
Section 903	Increased penalties for defrauding shareholders
Section 904	Increased penalties associated with a conviction
Section 905	US Sentencing Commission must review sentencing guidelines related to certain white collar crimes
Section 1102	Penalties for tampering with evidence and/or documents in an official proceeding
Section 1106	Maximum SEC penalty fine for individuals, corporations, entities is defined
Section 1107	Penalties for retaliation or discrimination against another person providing information to the SEC
Transparency: the state of openness or being free from pretense or deceit	
Section 102	Public accounting firms must submit reports to PCAOB, periodically and upon request
Section 301	Audit committee oversight of audit activities
Section 306	Guidelines and requirements for insider trading
Section 401	GAAP accounting principles must be used for filing financials
Section 402	Prohibition of personal loans from issuer to directors/officers
Section 403	Issuers must make stock purchase information available to the public
Section 404	Weaknesses in the effectiveness of the internal control over financial reporting must be reported by management to the registered public accounting firm
Section 409	Issuers must quickly disclose information about material changes in the financial conditions or operations to the public
Section 806	Whistleblower program must be established
Section 906	Directors/officers must certify every periodic report submitted to the SEC, or else face criminal penalties
Responsibility: the moral, legal, or mental obligation for a course of action or producing results	
Section 307	Ethical responsibilities of attorneys
Section 401	Issuer is responsible for disclosing complex transactions and pro forma figures
Section 403	Insiders must file periodic statements with the SEC
Section 406	Issuers must adopt a 'code of ethics' for directors/officers
Section 407	Issuers must disclose who is the financial expert of the audit committee to the SEC, or disclose why they have none
Section 501	Working environment for securities analysts must promote objectivity and independence
Section 803	Debts incurred as a result of criminal activity against Federal or State security laws will not be discharged
Section 805	US Sentencing Commission to revisit and update the sentences relating to obstruction of justice and extensive criminal fraud
Section 806	Whistleblower program must be established and communicated to all employees
Section 807	Criminal penalties for defrauding shareholders of publicly traded companies

Section 906	Directors/officers must certify every periodic report submitted to the SEC, or else face criminal penalties
Section 1001	CEO is individually accountable and responsible for financial reporting results
Section 1105	SEC authority to prohibit individuals from serving as directors/officers during cease-and-desist proceeding

Knowledge Areas identify the corporate resource or department that is most responsible for compliance with, or that implement, a particular SOX regulation. Areas of responsibility addressed in this Introduction include:

- **Accounting and Finance (A and F)** – Although the entire department(s) might participate in the design and implementation of specific controls, the Chief Financial Officer (CFO) or equivalent director or officer of the issuing company, would be ultimately held responsible for all actions taken by this Knowledge Area.
- **Information Technology (IT)** – The Chief Information Officer (CIO) or equivalent, and his or her staff are responsible for insuring the technological and systems security for the company.
- **Law, Ethics and Compliance (LEC)** – Activities undertaken by this Knowledge Area may actually bridge several different departments in the practitioner's company, involving legal counsel, human resources and compliance officers.
- **Internal/External Audit (IEA)** – Internal audit refers to those functional areas which actually carry out audit testing on behalf of management, or a department which oversees the issuer's self-audit activities. External audit is defined as the registered public accounting firm that is hired to issue an audit conclusion. These Knowledge Areas were combined for the purposes of this Introduction, to emphasize the close working relationship and overlapping responsibilities between the two.

Practitioners Perspective and Regulation Synopsis

This section provides an explanation of the Sarbanes-Oxley Act in terms meaningful to financial and business professionals faced with meeting the requirements of SOX. With the goal of being a single source of high-level SOX information, any references to other legislation, by the Security Exchange Commission and other government entities, have been summarized within the synopsis.

Generally Accepted SOX Principle [GASP]

This section explains the generally accepted SOX practice, and points out the practices or principles that translate into best practices and help a company become compliant. Since specific ways to comply with the SOX Act have not been, and are not likely to be, published by the PCAOB, the practitioner must discern the best way to attain compliance, according to the company's priorities, industry, risk factors and budget. This Introduction offers information about practices and principles that have helped many other companies comply with the SOX Act, and provides suggestions for the practitioner's consideration.

CHAPTER 1:
Public Company Accounting Oversight Board

Practitioners Perspective and Regulation Synopsis

Title 1 establishes the Public Company Accounting Oversight Board (PCAOB) as an agency of the US Government to oversee the audit of publicly traded companies.

- It is mandatory for all public accounting firms, which audit public companies, to register with the PCAOB.
- The PCAOB provides guidelines specific to auditing, quality control practices, independence standards, frequency and expected results of registered public accounting firm inspections.
- Lack of compliance with PCAOB guidelines will result in investigations and disciplinary proceedings of public accounting firms. Serious penalties can result if firms are non-complaint with the PCAOB directives and mandates.
- The Securities Exchange Commission oversees the PCAOB.
- Title 1 establishes the manner in which the PCAOB as well as the standards setting body are funded.
- The PCAOB is also referred to as the 'Board' in this publication.

Regulation Text

SEC. 101. ESTABLISHMENT; ADMINISTRATIVE PROVISIONS.

(a) ESTABLISHMENT OF BOARD.—There is established the Public Company Accounting Oversight Board, to oversee the audit of public companies that are subject to the securities laws, and related matters, in order to protect the interests of investors and further the public interest in

the preparation of informative, accurate, and independent audit reports for companies the securities of which are sold to, and held by and for, public investors. The Board shall be a body corporate, operate as a nonprofit corporation, and have succession until dissolved by an Act of Congress.
(b) STATUS.—The Board shall not be an agency or establishment of the United States Government and, except as otherwise provided in this Act, shall be subject to, and have all the powers conferred upon a nonprofit corporation by, the District of Columbia Nonprofit Corporation Act. No member or person employed by, or agent for, the Board shall be deemed to be an officer or employee of or agent for the Federal Government by reason of such service.

(c) DUTIES OF THE BOARD.—The Board shall, subject to action by the Commission under section 107, and once a determination is made by the Commission under subsection (d) of this section—
(1) register public accounting firms that prepare audit reports for issuers, in accordance with section 102;
(2) establish or adopt, or both, by rule, auditing, quality control, ethics, independence, and other standards relating to the preparation of audit reports for issuers, in accordance with section 103;
(3) conduct inspections of registered public accounting firms, in accordance with section 104 and the rules of the Board;
(4) conduct investigations and disciplinary proceedings concerning, and impose appropriate sanctions where justified upon, registered public accounting firms and associated persons of such firms, in accordance with section 105;
(5) perform such other duties or functions as the Board (or the Commission, by rule or order) determines are necessary or appropriate to promote high professional standards among, and improve the quality of audit services offered by, registered public accounting firms and associated persons thereof, or otherwise to carry out this Act, in order to protect investors, or to further the public interest;
(6) enforce compliance with this Act, the rules of the Board, professional standards, and the securities laws relating to the preparation and issuance of audit reports and the obligations and liabilities of accountants with respect thereto, by registered public accounting firms and associated persons thereof; and

(7) set the budget and manage the operations of the Board and the staff of the Board.

(d) COMMISSION DETERMINATION.—The members of the Board shall take such action (including hiring of staff, proposal of rules, and adoption of initial and transitional auditing and other professional standards) as may be necessary or appropriate to enable the Commission to determine, not later than 270 days after the date of enactment of this Act, that the Board is so organized and has the capacity to carry out the requirements of this title, and to enforce compliance with this title by registered public accounting firms and associated persons thereof. The Commission shall be responsible, prior to the appointment of the Board, for the planning for the establishment and administrative transition to the Board's operation.

(e) BOARD MEMBERSHIP.—
 (1) COMPOSITION.—The Board shall have 5 members, appointed from among prominent individuals of integrity and reputation who have a demonstrated commitment to the interests of investors and the public, and an understanding of the responsibilities for and nature of the financial disclosures required of issuers under the securities laws and the obligations of accountants with respect to the preparation and issuance of audit reports with respect to such disclosures.
 (2) LIMITATION.—Two members, and only 2 members, of the Board shall be or have been certified public accountants pursuant to the laws of 1 or more States, provided that, if 1 of those 2 members is the chairperson, he or she may not have been a practicing certified public accountant for at least 5 years prior to his or her appointment to the Board.
 (3) FULL-TIME INDEPENDENT SERVICE.—Each member of the Board shall serve on a full-time basis, and may not, concurrent with service on the Board, be employed by any other person or engage in any other professional or business activity. No member of the Board may share in any of the profits of, or receive payments from, a public accounting firm (or any other person, as determined by rule of the Commission), other than fixed continuing payments, and subject to such conditions as the Commission may impose, under standard arrangements for the retirement of members of public accounting firms.

(4) APPOINTMENT OF BOARD MEMBERS.—
　(A) INITIAL BOARD.—Not later than 90 days after the date of enactment of this Act, the Commission, after consultation with the Chairman of the Board of Governors of the Federal Reserve System and the Secretary of the Treasury, shall appoint the chairperson and other initial members of the Board, and shall designate a term of service for each.
　(B) VACANCIES.—A vacancy on the Board shall not affect the powers of the Board, but shall be filled in the same manner as provided for appointments under this section.
(5) TERM OF SERVICE.—
　(A) IN GENERAL.—The term of service of each Board member shall be 5 years, and until a successor is appointed, except that—
　　(i) the terms of office of the initial Board members (other than the chairperson) shall expire in annual increments, 1 on each of the first 4 anniversaries of the initial date of appointment; and
　　(ii) any Board member appointed to fill a vacancy occurring before the expiration of the term for which the predecessor was appointed shall be appointed only for the remainder of that term.
　(B) TERM LIMITATION.—No person may serve as a member of the Board, or as chairperson of the Board, for more than 2 terms, whether or not such terms of service are consecutive.
(6) REMOVAL FROM OFFICE.—A member of the Board may be removed by the Commission from office, in accordance with section 107(d)(3), for good cause shown before the expiration of the term of that member.

(f) POWERS OF THE BOARD.—In addition to any authority granted to the Board otherwise in this Act, the Board shall have the power, subject to section 107—
　(1) to sue and be sued, complain and defend, in its corporate name and through its own counsel, with the approval of the Commission, in any Federal, State, or other court;
　(2) to conduct its operations and maintain offices, and to exercise all other rights and powers authorized by this Act, in any State, without regard to any qualification, licensing, or other provision of law in effect in such State (or a political subdivision thereof);

(3) to lease, purchase, accept gifts or donations of or otherwise acquire, improve, use, sell, exchange, or convey, all of or an interest in any property, wherever situated;

(4) to appoint such employees, accountants, attorneys, and other agents as may be necessary or appropriate, and to determine their qualifications, define their duties, and fix their salaries or other compensation (at a level that is comparable to private sector self-regulatory, accounting, technical, supervisory, or other staff or management positions);

(5) to allocate, assess, and collect accounting support fees established pursuant to section 109, for the Board, and other fees and charges imposed under this title; and

(6) to enter into contracts, execute instruments, incur liabilities, and do any and all other acts and things necessary, appropriate, or incidental to the conduct of its operations and the exercise of its obligations, rights, and powers imposed or granted by this title.

(g) RULES OF THE BOARD.—The rules of the Board shall, subject to the approval of the Commission—

(1) Provide for the operation and administration of the Board, the exercise of its authority, and the performance of its responsibilities under this Act;

(2) Permit, as the Board determines necessary or appropriate, delegation by the Board of any of its functions to an individual member or employee of the Board, or to a division of the Board, including functions with respect to hearing, determining, ordering, certifying, reporting, or otherwise acting as to any matter, except that—

(A) the Board shall retain a discretionary right to review any action pursuant to any such delegated function, upon its own motion;

(B) a person shall be entitled to a review by the Board with respect to any matter so delegated, and the decision of the Board upon such review shall be deemed to be the action of the Board for all purposes (including appeal or review thereof); and

(C) if the right to exercise a review described in subparagraph (A) is declined, or if no such review is sought within the time stated in the rules of the Board, then the action taken by the holder of such delegation shall for all purposes, including appeal or review thereof, be deemed to be the action of the Board;

(3) Establish ethics rules and standards of conduct for Board members and staff, including a bar on practice before the Board (and the Commission, with respect to Board-related matters) of 1 year for former members of the Board, and appropriate periods (not to exceed 1 year) for former staff of the Board;
and
(4) Provide as otherwise required by this Act.

(h) ANNUAL REPORT TO THE COMMISSION.—The Board shall submit an annual report (including its audited financial statements) to the Commission, and the Commission shall transmit a copy of that report to the Committee on Banking, Housing, and Urban Affairs of the Senate, and the Committee on Financial Services of the House of Representatives, not later than 30 days after the date of receipt of that report by the Commission.

SEC. 102. REGISTRATION WITH THE BOARD.
(a) MANDATORY REGISTRATION.—Beginning 180 days after the date of the determination of the Commission under section 101(d), it shall be unlawful for any person that is not a registered public accounting firm to prepare or issue, or to participate in the preparation or issuance of, any audit report with respect to any issuer.

(b) APPLICATIONS FOR REGISTRATION.—
   (1) FORM OF APPLICATION.—A public accounting firm shall use such form as the Board may prescribe, by rule, to apply for registration under this section.
   (2) CONTENTS OF APPLICATIONS.—Each public accounting firm shall submit, as part of its application for registration, in such detail as the Board shall specify—
      (A) The names of all issuers for which the firm prepared or issued audit reports during the immediately preceding calendar year, and for which the firm expects to prepare or issue audit reports during the current calendar year; (15 USC 7212).
      (B) The annual fees received by the firm from each such issuer for audit services, other accounting services, and non-audit services, respectively;

(C) Such other current financial information for the most recently completed fiscal year of the firm as the Board may reasonably request;

(D) A statement of the quality control policies of the firm for its accounting and auditing practices;

(E) A list of all accountants associated with the firm who participate in or contribute to the preparation of audit reports, stating the license or certification number of each such person, as well as the State license numbers of the firm itself;

(F) Information relating to criminal, civil, or administrative actions or disciplinary proceedings pending against the firm or any associated person of the firm in connection with any audit report;

(G) Copies of any periodic or annual disclosure filed by an issuer with the Commission during the immediately preceding calendar year which discloses accounting disagreements between such issuer and the firm in connection with an audit report furnished or prepared by the firm for such issuer; and

(H) Such other information as the rules of the Board or the Commission shall specify as necessary or appropriate in the public interest or for the protection of investors.

(3) CONSENTS.—Each application for registration under this subsection shall include—

(A) a consent executed by the public accounting firm to co-operation in and compliance with any request for testimony or the production of documents made by the Board in the furtherance of its authority and responsibilities under this title and an agreement to secure and enforce similar consents from each of the associated persons of the public accounting firm as a condition of their continued employment by or other association with such firm.

(B) a statement that such firm understands and agrees that co-operation and compliance, as described in the consent required by subparagraph (A), and the securing and enforcement of such consents from its associated persons, in accordance with the rules of the Board, shall be a condition to the continuing effectiveness of the registration of the firm with the Board.

(c) ACTION ON APPLICATIONS.—
(1) TIMING.—The Board shall approve a completed application for registration not later than 45 days after the date of receipt of the application, in accordance with the rules of the Board, unless the Board, prior to such date, issues a written notice of disapproval to, or requests more information from, the prospective registrant.
(2) TREATMENT.—A written notice of disapproval of a completed application under paragraph (1) for registration shall be treated as a disciplinary sanction for purposes of sections 105(d) and 107(c).

(d) PERIODIC REPORTS.—Each registered public accounting firm shall submit an annual report to the Board, and may be required to report more frequently, as necessary to update the information contained in its application for registration under this section, and to provide to the Board such additional information as the Board or the Commission may specify, in accordance with subsection (b) (2).

(e) PUBLIC AVAILABILITY.—Registration applications and annual reports required by this subsection, or such portions of such applications or reports as may be designated under rules of the Board, shall be made available for public inspection, subject to rules of the Board or the Commission, and to applicable laws relating to the confidentiality of proprietary, personal, or other information contained in such applications or reports, provided that, in all events, the Board shall protect from public disclosure information reasonably identified by the subject accounting firm as proprietary information.

(f) REGISTRATION AND ANNUAL FEES.—The Board shall assess and collect a registration fee and an annual fee from each registered public accounting firm, in amounts that are sufficient to recover the costs of processing and reviewing applications and annual reports.

SEC. 103. AUDITING, QUALITY CONTROL, AND INDEPENDENCE STANDARDS AND RULES.

(a) AUDITING, QUALITY CONTROL, AND ETHICS STANDARDS.—

(1) IN GENERAL.—The Board shall, by rule, establish, including, to the extent it determines appropriate, through adoption of standards proposed by 1 or more professional groups of accountants designated pursuant to paragraph (3)(A) or advisory groups convened pursuant to paragraph (4), and amend or otherwise modify or alter, such auditing and related attestation standards, such quality control standards, and such ethics standards to be used by registered public accounting firms in the preparation and issuance of audit reports, as required by this Act or the rules of the Commission, or as may be necessary or appropriate in the public interest or for the protection of investors.

(2) RULE REQUIREMENTS.—In carrying out paragraph (1), the Board—

(A) Shall include in the auditing standards that it adopts, requirements that each registered public accounting firm shall—

(i) prepare, and maintain for a period of not less than 7 years, audit work papers, and other information related to any audit report, in sufficient detail to support the conclusions reached in such report;

(ii) provide a concurring or second partner review and approval of such audit report (and other related information), and concurring approval in its issuance, by a qualified person (as prescribed by the Board) associated with the public accounting firm, other than the person in charge of the audit, or by an independent reviewer (as prescribed by the Board); and (iii) describe in each audit report the scope of the auditor's testing of the internal control structure and procedures of the issuer, required by section 404(b), and present in such report or in a separate report

(I) the findings of the auditor from such testing;

(II) an evaluation of whether such internal control structure and procedures—

(aa) include maintenance of records that in reasonable detail accurately and fairly reflect the transactions and dispositions of the assets of the issuer;

(bb) provide reasonable assurance that transactions are recorded as necessary to permit preparation of financial statements in accordance with generally accepted accounting principles, and that receipts and expenditures of the issuer are being made only in accordance with authorizations of management and directors of the issuer; and

(III) a description, at a minimum, of material weaknesses in such internal controls, and of any material noncompliance found on the basis of such testing.

(B) Shall include, in the quality control standards that it adopts with respect to the issuance of audit reports, requirements for every registered public accounting firm relating to—

(i) monitoring of professional ethics and independence from issuers on behalf of which the firm issues audit reports;

(ii) consultation within such firm on accounting and auditing questions;

(iii) supervision of audit work;

(iv) hiring, professional development, and advancement of personnel;

(v) the acceptance and continuation of engagements;

(vi) internal inspection; and

(vii) such other requirements as the Board may prescribe, subject to subsection (a) (1).

(3) AUTHORITY TO ADOPT OTHER STANDARDS.—

(A) IN GENERAL.—In carrying out this subsection, the Board—

(i) may adopt as its rules, subject to the terms of section 107, any portion of any statement of auditing standards or other professional standards that the Board determines satisfy the requirements of paragraph

(1), and that were proposed by 1 or more professional groups of accountants that shall be designated or recognized by the Board, by rule, for such purpose, pursuant to this paragraph or 1 or more advisory groups convened pursuant to paragraph (4); and

(ii) notwithstanding clause (i), shall retain full authority to modify, supplement, revise, or subsequently amend, modify, or repeal, in whole or in part, any portion of any statement described in clause (i).

(B) INITIAL AND TRANSITIONAL STANDARDS.—The Board shall adopt standards described in subparagraph (A) (i) as initial or transitional standards, to the extent the Board determines necessary, prior to a determination of the Commission under section 101(d), and such standards shall be separately approved by the Commission at the time of that determination, without regard to the procedures required by section 107 that otherwise would apply to the approval of rules of the Board.

(4) ADVISORY GROUPS.—The Board shall convene, or authorize its staff to convene, such expert advisory groups as may be appropriate, which may include practicing accountants and other experts, as well as representatives of other interested groups, subject to such rules as the Board may prescribe to prevent conflicts of interest, to make recommendations concerning the content (including proposed drafts) of auditing, quality control, ethics, independence, or other standards required to be established under this section.

(b) INDEPENDENCE STANDARDS AND RULES.—The Board shall establish such rules as may be necessary or appropriate in the public interest or for the protection of investors, to implement, or as authorized under, title II of this Act.

(c) CO-OPERATION WITH DESIGNATED PROFESSIONAL GROUPS OF ACCOUNTANTS AND ADVISORY GROUPS.—

(1) IN GENERAL.—The Board shall co-operate on an ongoing basis with professional groups of accountants designated under subsection (a) (3) (A) and advisory groups convened under subsection (a)(4) In the examination of the need for changes in any standards subject to its authority under subsection (a), recommend issues for inclusion on the agendas of such designated professional groups of accountants or advisory groups, and take such other steps as it deems appropriate to increase the effectiveness of the standard setting process.

(2) BOARD RESPONSES.—The Board shall respond in a timely fashion to requests from designated professional groups of accountants and advisory groups referred to in paragraph (1) for any changes in standards over which the Board has authority.

(d) EVALUATION OF STANDARD SETTING PROCESS.—The Board shall include in the annual report required by section 101(h) the results of its standard setting responsibilities during the period to which the report relates, including a discussion of the work of the Board with any designated professional groups of accountants and advisory groups described in paragraphs (3) (A) and (4) of subsection (a), and its pending issues agenda for future standard setting projects.

SEC. 104. INSPECTIONS OF REGISTERED PUBLIC ACCOUNTING FIRMS.

(a) IN GENERAL.—The Board shall conduct a continuing program of inspections to assess the degree of compliance of each registered public accounting firm and associated persons of that firm with this Act, the rules of the Board, the rules of the Commission, or professional standards, in connection with its performance of audits, issuance of audit reports, and related matters involving issuers.

(b) INSPECTION FREQUENCY.—
    (1) IN GENERAL.—Subject to paragraph (2), inspections required by this section shall be conducted:
        (A) Annually with respect to each registered public accounting firm that regularly provides audit reports for more than 100 issuers; and
        (B) Not less frequently than once every 3 years with respect to each registered public accounting firm that regularly provides audit reports for 100 or fewer issuers.
    (2) ADJUSTMENTS TO SCHEDULES.—The Board may, by rule, adjust the inspection schedules set under paragraph (1) if the Board finds that different inspection schedules are consistent with the purposes of this Act, the public interest, and the protection of investors. The Board may conduct special inspections at the request of the Commission or upon its own motion.

(c) PROCEDURES.—The Board shall, in each inspection under this section, and in accordance with its rules for such inspections.

(1) identify any act or practice or omission to act by the registered public accounting firm, or by any associated person thereof, revealed by such inspection that may be in violation of this Act, the rules of the Board, the rules of the Commission, the firm's own quality control policies, or professional standards;

(2) report any such act, practice, or omission, if appropriate, to the Commission and each appropriate State regulatory authority; and

(3) begin a formal investigation or take disciplinary action, if appropriate, with respect to any such violation, in accordance with this Act and the rules of the Board.

(d) CONDUCT OF INSPECTIONS.—In conducting an inspection of a registered public accounting firm under this section, the Board shall:

(1) inspect and review selected audit and review engagements of the firm (which may include audit engagements that are the subject of ongoing litigation or other controversy between the firm and 1 or more third parties), performed at various offices and by various associated persons of the firm, as selected by the Board;

(2) evaluate the sufficiency of the quality control system of the firm, and the manner of the documentation and communication of that system by the firm; and

(3) perform such other testing of the audit, supervisory, and quality control procedures of the firm as are necessary or appropriate in light of the purpose of the inspection and the responsibilities of the Board.

(e) RECORD RETENTION.—The rules of the Board may require the retention by registered public accounting firms for inspection purposes of records whose retention is not otherwise required by section 103 or the rules issued thereunder.

(f) PROCEDURES FOR REVIEW.—The rules of the Board shall provide a procedure for the review of and response to a draft inspection report by the registered public accounting firm under inspection. The Board shall take such action with respect to such response as it considers appropriate (including revising the draft report or continuing or supplementing its inspection activities before issuing a final report), but the text of any such response, appropriately reacted to protect information reasonably identified by the accounting firm as confidential, shall be attached to and made part of the inspection report.

(g) REPORT.—A written report of the findings of the Board for each inspection under this section, subject to subsection (h), shall be:
   (1) transmitted, in appropriate detail, to the Commission and each appropriate State regulatory authority, accompanied by any letter or comments by the Board or the inspector, and any letter of response from the registered public accounting firm;
   (2) made available in appropriate detail to the public (subject to section 105(b)(5)(A), and to the protection of such confidential and proprietary information as the Board may determine to be appropriate, or as may be required by law), except that no portions of the inspection report that deal with criticisms of or potential defects in the quality control systems of the firm under inspection shall be made public if those criticisms or defects are addressed by the firm, to the satisfaction of the Board, not later than 12 months after the date of the inspection report.

(h) INTERIM COMMISSION REVIEW.—
   (1) REVIEWABLE MATTERS.—A registered public accounting firm may seek review by the Commission, pursuant to such rules as the Commission shall promulgate, if the firm—
      (A) has provided the Board with a response, pursuant to rules issued by the Board under subsection (f), to the substance of particular items in a draft inspection report, and disagrees with the assessments contained in any final report prepared by the Board following such response; or
      (B) disagrees with the determination of the Board that criticisms or defects identified in an inspection report have not been addressed to the satisfaction of the Board within 12 months of the date of the inspection report, for purposes of subsection (g)(2).
   (2) TREATMENT OF REVIEW.—Any decision of the Commission with respect to a review under paragraph (1) shall not be reviewable under section 25 of the Securities Exchange Act of 1934 (15 U.S.C. 78y), or deemed to be "final agency action" for purposes of section 704 of title 5, United States Code.

(3) TIMING.—Review under paragraph (1) may be sought during the 30-day period following the date of the event giving rise to the review under subparagraph (A) or (B) of paragraph (1).

SEC. 105. INVESTIGATIONS AND DISCIPLINARY PROCEEDINGS.
(a) IN GENERAL.—The Board shall establish, by rule, subject to the requirements of this section, fair procedures for the investigation and disciplining of registered public accounting firms and associated persons of such firms.

(b) INVESTIGATIONS.—
   (1) AUTHORITY.—In accordance with the rules of the Board, the Board may conduct an investigation of any act or practice, or omission to act, by a registered public accounting firm, any associated person of such firm, or both, that may violate any provision of this Act, the rules of the Board, the provisions of the securities laws relating to the preparation and issuance of audit reports and the obligations and liabilities of accountants with respect thereto, including the rules of the Commission issued under this Act, or professional standards, regardless of how the act, practice, or omission is brought to the attention of the Board.
   (2) TESTIMONY AND DOCUMENT PRODUCTION.—In addition to such other actions as the Board determines to be necessary or appropriate, the rules of the Board may;
      (A) require the testimony of the firm or of any person associated with a registered public accounting firm, with respect to any matter that the Board considers relevant or material to an investigation;
      (B) require the production of audit work papers and any other document or information in the possession of a registered public accounting firm or any associated person thereof, wherever domiciled, that the Board considers relevant or material to the investigation, and may inspect the books and records of such firm or associated person to verify the accuracy of any documents or information supplied;
      (C) request the testimony of, and production of any document in the possession of, any other person, including any client of a registered public accounting firm that the Board considers relevant or material to an investigation under this section, with appropriate notice, subject

to the needs of the investigation, as permitted under the rules of the Board; and

(D) provide for procedures to seek issuance by the Commission, in a manner established by the Commission, of a subpoena to require the testimony of, and production of any document in the possession of, any person, including any client of a registered public accounting firm that the Board considers relevant or material to an investigation under this section.

(3) NONCO-OPERATION WITH INVESTIGATIONS.—

(A) IN GENERAL.—If a registered public accounting firm or any associated person thereof refuses to testify, produce documents, or otherwise co-operate with the Board in connection with an investigation under this section, the Board may;

(i) suspend or bar such person from being associated with a registered public accounting firm, or require the registered public accounting firm to end such association;

(ii) suspend or revoke the registration of the public accounting firm; and

(iii) invoke such other lesser sanctions as the Board considers appropriate, and as specified by rule of the Board.

(B) PROCEDURE.—Any action taken by the Board under this paragraph shall be subject to the terms of section 107(c).

(4) CO-ORDINATION AND REFERRAL OF INVESTIGATIONS.—

(A) CO-ORDINATION.—The Board shall notify the Commission of any pending Board investigation involving a potential violation of the securities laws, and thereafter co-ordinate its work with the work of the Commission's Division of Enforcement, as necessary to protect an ongoing Commission investigation.

(B) REFERRAL.—The Board may refer an investigation under this section—

(i) to the Commission;

(ii) to any other Federal functional regulator (as defined in section 509 of the Gramm-Leach-Bliley Act (15 U.S.C. 6809)), in the case of an investigation that concerns an audit report for an institution that is subject to the jurisdiction of such regulator; and (iii) at the direction of the Commission, to—

(I) the Attorney General of the United States;
(II) the attorney general of 1 or more States; and
(III) the appropriate State regulatory authority

(5) USE OF DOCUMENTS.—
(A) CONFIDENTIALITY.—Except as provided in subparagraph (B), all documents and information prepared or received by or specifically for the Board, and deliberations of the Board and its employees and agents, in connection with an inspection under section 104 or with an investigation under this section, shall be confidential and privileged as an evidentiary matter (and shall not be subject to civil discovery or other legal process) in any proceeding in any Federal or State court or administrative agency, and shall be exempt from disclosure, in the hands of an agency or establishment of the Federal Government, under the Freedom of Information Act (5 U.S.C. 552a), or otherwise, unless and until presented in connection with a public proceeding or released in accordance with subsection (c).
(B) AVAILABILITY TO GOVERNMENT AGENCIES.—Without the loss of its status as confidential and privileged in the hands of the Board, all information referred to in subparagraph (A) may;
(i) be made available to the Commission; and
(ii) in the discretion of the Board, when determined by the Board to be necessary to accomplish the purposes of this Act or to protect investors, be made available to—
(I) the Attorney General of the United States;
(II) the appropriate Federal functional regulator (as defined in section 509 of the Gramm-Leach-Bliley Act (15 U.S.C. 6809)), other than the Commission, with respect to an audit report for an institution subject to the jurisdiction of such regulator;
(III) State attorneys general in connection with any criminal investigation; and
(IV) any appropriate State regulatory authority, each of which shall maintain such information as confidential and privileged.
(6) IMMUNITY.—Any employee of the Board engaged in carrying out an investigation under this Act shall be immune from any civil liability arising out of such investigation in the same manner and to the same extent as an employee of the Federal Government in similar circumstances.

(c) DISCIPLINARY PROCEDURES.—

(1) NOTIFICATION; RECORDKEEPING.—The rules of the Board shall provide that in any proceeding by the Board to determine whether a registered public accounting firm, or an associated person thereof, should be disciplined, the Board shall—

(A) Bring specific charges with respect to the firm or associated person;

(B) Notify such firm or associated person of, and provide to the firm or associated person an opportunity to defend against, such charges; and

(C) Keep a record of the proceedings.

(2) PUBLIC HEARINGS.—Hearings under this section shall not be public, unless otherwise ordered by the Board for good cause shown, with the consent of the parties to such hearing.

(3) SUPPORTING STATEMENT.—A determination by the Board to impose a sanction under this subsection shall be supported by a statement setting forth—

(A) Each act or practice in which the registered public accounting firm, or associated person, has engaged (or omitted to engage), or that forms a basis for all or a part of such sanction;

(B) The specific provision of this Act, the securities laws, the rules of the Board, or professional standards which the Board determines has been violated; and (C) the sanction imposed, including a justification for that sanction.

(4) SANCTIONS.—If the Board finds, based on all of the facts and circumstances, that a registered public accounting firm or associated person thereof has engaged in any act or practice, or omitted to act, in violation of this Act, the rules of the Board, the provisions of the securities laws relating to the preparation and issuance of audit reports and the obligations and liabilities of accountants with respect thereto, including the rules of the Commission issued under this Act, or professional standards, the Board may impose such disciplinary or remedial sanctions as it determines appropriate, subject to applicable limitations under paragraph (5), including—

(A) Temporary suspension or permanent revocation of registration under this title;

(B) Temporary or permanent suspension or bar of a person from further association with any registered public accounting firm;

(C) Temporary or permanent limitation on the activities, functions, or operations of such firm or person (other than in connection with required additional professional education or training);

(D) A civil money penalty for each such violation, in an amount equal to—

(i) not more than $100,000 for a natural person or $2,000,000 for any other person; and

(ii) in any case to which paragraph (5) applies, not more than $750,000 for a natural person or $15,000,000 for any other person;

(E) Censure;

(F) Required additional professional education or training; or

(G) Any other appropriate sanction provided for in the rules of the Board.

(5) INTENTIONAL OR OTHER KNOWING CONDUCT.—The sanctions and penalties described in subparagraphs (A) through (C) and (D) (ii) of paragraph (4) shall only apply to—

(A) intentional or knowing conduct, including reckless conduct, that results in violation of the applicable statutory, regulatory, or professional standard; or

(B) repeated instances of negligent conduct, each resulting in a violation of the applicable statutory, regulatory, or professional standard.

(6) FAILURE TO SUPERVISE.—

(A) IN GENERAL.—The Board may impose sanctions under this section on a registered accounting firm or upon the supervisory personnel of such firm, if the Board finds that—

(i) the firm has failed reasonably to supervise an associated person, either as required by the rules of the Board relating to auditing or quality control standards, or otherwise, with a view to preventing violations of this Act, the rules of the Board, the provisions of the securities laws relating to the preparation and issuance of audit reports and the obligations and liabilities of accountants with respect thereto, including the rules of the Commission under this Act, or professional standards; and

(ii) such associated person commits a violation of this Act, or any of such rules, laws, or standards.

(B) RULE OF CONSTRUCTION.—No associated person of a registered public accounting firm shall be deemed to have failed reasonably to supervise any other person for purposes of subparagraph (A), if;

(i) there have been established in and for that firm procedures, and a system for applying such procedures, that comply with applicable rules of the Board and that would reasonably be expected to prevent and detect any such violation by such associated person; and

(ii) such person has reasonably discharged the duties and obligations incumbent upon that person by reason of such procedures and system, and had no reasonable cause to believe that such procedures and system were not being complied with.

(7) EFFECT OF SUSPENSION

(A) ASSOCIATION WITH A PUBLIC ACCOUNTING FIRM. It shall be unlawful for any person that is suspended or barred from being associated with a registered public accounting firm under this subsection willfully to become or remain associated with any registered public accounting firm, or for any registered public accounting firm that knew, or, in the exercise of reasonable care should have known, of the suspension or bar, to permit such an association, without the consent of the Board or the Commission.

(B) ASSOCIATION WITH AN ISSUER.—It shall be unlawful for any person that is suspended or barred from being associated with an issuer under this subsection willfully to become or remain associated with any issuer in an accountancy or a financial management capacity, and for any issuer that knew, or in the exercise of reasonable care should have known, of such suspension or bar, to permit such an association, without the consent of the Board or the Commission.

(d) REPORTING OF SANCTIONS.—

(1) RECIPIENTS.—If the Board imposes a disciplinary sanction, in accordance with this section, the Board shall report the sanction to:

(A) the Commission;

(B) any appropriate State regulatory authority or any foreign accountancy licensing board with which such firm or person is licensed or certified; and

(C) the public (once any stay on the imposition of such sanction has been lifted).

(2) CONTENTS.—The information reported under paragraph (1) shall include—
- (A) the name of the sanctioned person;
- (B) a description of the sanction and the basis for its imposition; and
- (C) such other information as the Board deems appropriate.

(e) STAY OF SANCTIONS.

(1) IN GENERAL.—Application to the Commission for review, or the institution by the Commission of review, of any disciplinary action of the Board shall operate as a stay of any such disciplinary action, unless and until the Commission orders (summarily or after notice and opportunity for hearing on the question of a stay, which hearing may consist solely of the submission of affidavits or presentation of oral arguments) that no such stay shall continue to operate.

(2) EXPEDITED PROCEDURES.—The Commission shall establish for appropriate cases an expedited procedure for consideration and determination of the question of the duration of a stay pending review of any disciplinary action of the Board under this subsection.

SEC. 106. FOREIGN PUBLIC ACCOUNTING FIRMS.

(a) APPLICABILITY TO CERTAIN FOREIGN FIRMS.

(1) IN GENERAL.—Any foreign public accounting firm that prepares or furnishes an audit report with respect to any issuer, shall be subject to this Act and the rules of the Board and the Commission issued under this Act, in the same manner and to the same extent as a public accounting firm that is organized and operates under the laws of the United States or any State, except that registration pursuant to section 102 shall not by itself provide a basis for subjecting such a foreign public accounting firm to the jurisdiction of the Federal or State courts, other than with respect to controversies between such firms and the Board.

(2) BOARD AUTHORITY.—The Board may, by rule, determine that a foreign public accounting firm (or a class of such firms) that does not issue audit reports nonetheless plays such a substantial role in the preparation and furnishing of such reports for particular issuers, that it is necessary or appropriate, in light of the purposes of this Act and in the public interest or for the protection of investors, that such firm (or class of firms) should be treated as a public accounting firm (or firms) for purposes of registration under, and oversight by the Board in accordance with, this title.

(b) PRODUCTION OF AUDIT WORKPAPERS.
(1) CONSENT BY FOREIGN FIRMS.—If a foreign public accounting firm issues an opinion or otherwise performs material services upon which a registered public accounting firm relies in issuing all or part of any audit report or any opinion contained in an audit report, that foreign public accounting firm shall be deemed to have consented:
(A) To produce its audit workpapers for the Board or the Commission in connection with any investigation by either body with respect to that audit report; and
(B) To be subject to the jurisdiction of the courts of the United States for purposes of enforcement of any request for production of such workpapers.
(2) CONSENT BY DOMESTIC FIRMS.—A registered public accounting firm that relies upon the opinion of a foreign public accounting firm, as described in paragraph (1).
(A) To have consented to supplying the audit workpapers of that foreign public accounting firm in response to a request for production by the Board or the Commission; and
(B) To have secured the agreement of that foreign public accounting firm to such production, as a condition of its reliance on the opinion of that foreign public accounting firm.

(c) EXEMPTION AUTHORITY.—The Commission, and the Board, subject to the approval of the Commission, may, by rule, regulation, or order, and as the Commission (or Board) determines necessary or appropriate in the public interest or for the protection of investors, either unconditionally or upon specified terms and conditions exempt any foreign public accounting firm, or any class of such firms, from any provision of this Act or the rules of the Board or the Commission issued under this Act.

(d) DEFINITION.—In this section, the term "foreign public accounting firm" means a public accounting firm that is organized and operates under the laws of a foreign government or political subdivision thereof.

SEC. 107. COMMISSION OVERSIGHT OF THE BOARD.

(a) GENERAL OVERSIGHT RESPONSIBILITY.—The Commission shall have oversight and enforcement authority over the Board, as provided in this Act. The provisions of section 17(a) (1) of the Securities Exchange Act of 1934 (15 U.S.C. 78q (a) (1)), and of section 17(b) (1) of the Securities Exchange Act of 1934 (15 U.S.C. 78q (b) (1)) shall apply to the Board as fully as if the Board were a "registered securities association" for purposes of those sections 17(a) (1) and 17(b) (1).

(b) RULES OF THE BOARD.—
    (1) DEFINITION.—In this section, the term "proposed rule" means any proposed rule of the Board, and any modification of any such rule.
    (2) PRIOR APPROVAL REQUIRED.—No rule of the Board shall become effective without prior approval of the Commission in accordance with this section, other than as provided in section 103(a)(3)(B) with respect to initial or transitional standards.
    (3) APPROVAL CRITERIA.—The Commission shall approve a proposed rule, if it finds that the rule is consistent with the requirements of this Act and the securities laws, or is necessary or appropriate in the public interest or for the protection of investors.
    (4) PROPOSED RULE PROCEDURES.—the provisions of paragraphs (1) through (3) of section 19(b) of the Securities Exchange Act of 1934 (15 U.S.C. 78s (b)) shall govern the proposed rules of the Board, as fully as if the Board were a "registered securities association" for purposes of that section 19(b), except that, for purposes of this paragraph—
        (A) the phrase "consistent with the requirements of this title and the rules and regulations there under applicable to such organization" in section 19(b) (2) of that Act shall be deemed to read "consistent with the requirements of title I of the Sarbanes-Oxley Act of 2002, and the rules and regulations issued there under applicable to such organization, or as necessary or appropriate in the public interest or for the protection of investors"; and
        (B) the phrase "otherwise in furtherance of the purposes of this title" in section 19(b) (3) (C) of that Act shall be deemed to read "otherwise in furtherance of the purposes of title I of the Sarbanes-Oxley Act of 2002".

(5) COMMISSION AUTHORITY TO AMEND RULES OF THE BOARD.—

The provisions of section 19(c) of the Securities Exchange Act of 1934 (15 U.S.C. 78s(c)) shall govern the abrogation, deletion, or addition to portions of the rules of the Board by the Commission as fully as if the Board were a "registered securities association" for purposes of that section 19(c), except that the phrase "to conform its rules to the requirements of this title and the rules and regulations there under applicable to such organization, or otherwise in furtherance of the purposes of this title" in section 19(c) of that Act shall, for purposes of this paragraph, be deemed to read "to assure the fair administration of the Public Company Accounting Oversight Board, conform the rules promulgated by that Board to the requirements of title I of the Sarbanes-Oxley Act of 2002, or otherwise further the purposes of that Act, the securities laws, and the rules and regulations there under applicable to that Board".

(c) COMMISSION REVIEW OF DISCIPLINARY ACTION TAKEN BY THE BOARD.—

(1) NOTICE OF SANCTION.—The Board shall promptly file notice with the Commission of any final sanction on any registered public accounting firm or on any associated person thereof, in such form and containing such information as the Commission, by rule, may prescribe.

(2) REVIEW OF SANCTIONS.—The provisions of sections 19(d)(2) and 19(e)(1) of the Securities Exchange Act of 1934 (15 U.S.C. 78s (d)(2) and (e)(1)) shall govern the review by the Commission of final disciplinary sanctions imposed by the Board (including sanctions imposed under section 105(b)(3) of this Act for non-co-operation in an investigation of the Board), as fully as if the Board were a self-regulatory organization and the Commission were the appropriate regulatory agency for such organization for purposes of those sections 19(d)(2) and 19(e)(1), except that, for purposes of this paragraph—

(A) section 105(e) of this Act (rather than that section 19(d)(2)) shall govern the extent to which application for, or institution by the Commission on its own motion of, review of any disciplinary action of the Board operates as a stay of such action;

(B) references in that section 19(e)(1) to "members" of such an organization shall be deemed to be references to registered public accounting firms;

(C) the phrase "consistent with the purposes of this title" in that section 19(e)(1) shall be deemed to read "consistent with the purposes of this title and title I of the Sarbanes-Oxley Act of 2002";

(D) references to rules of the Municipal Securities Rulemaking Board in that section 19(e)(1) shall not apply; and (E) the reference to section 19(e)(2) of the Securities Exchange Act of 1934 shall refer instead to section 107(c)(3) of this Act.

(3) COMMISSION MODIFICATION AUTHORITY.—The Commission may enhance, modify, cancel, reduce, or require the remission of a sanction imposed by the Board upon a registered public accounting firm or associated person thereof, if the Commission, having due regard for the public interest and the protection of investors, finds, after a proceeding in accordance with this subsection, that the sanction—

(A) is not necessary or appropriate in furtherance of this Act or the securities laws; or

(B) is excessive, oppressive, inadequate, or otherwise not appropriate to the finding or the basis on which the sanction was imposed.

(d) CENSURE OF THE BOARD; OTHER SANCTIONS.—

(1) RESCISSION OF BOARD AUTHORITY.—The Commission, by rule, consistent with the public interest, the protection of investors, and the other purposes of this Act and the securities laws, may relieve the Board of any responsibility to enforce compliance with any provision of this Act, the securities laws, the rules of the Board, or professional standards.

(2) CENSURE OF THE BOARD; LIMITATIONS.—The Commission may, by order, as it determines necessary or appropriate in the public interest, for the protection of investors, or otherwise in furtherance of the purposes of this Act or the securities laws, censure or impose limitations upon the activities, functions, and operations of the Board, if the Commission finds, on the record, after notice and opportunity for a hearing, that the Board;

(A) Has violated or is unable to comply with any provision of this Act, the rules of the Board, or the securities laws; or

(B) Without reasonable justification or excuse, has failed to enforce compliance with any such provision or rule, or any professional standard by a registered public accounting firm or an associated person thereof.

(3) CENSURE OF BOARD MEMBERS; REMOVAL FROM OFFICE.—The Commission may, as necessary or appropriate in the public interest, for the protection of investors, or otherwise in furtherance of the purposes of this Act or the securities laws, remove from office or censure any member of the Board, if the Commission finds, on the record, after notice and opportunity for a hearing, that such member;

(A) Has willfully violated any provision of this Act, the rules of the Board, or the securities laws;

(B) Has willfully abused the authority of that member; or

(C) Without reasonable justification or excuse, has failed to enforce compliance with any such provision or rule, or any professional standard by any registered public accounting firm or any associated person thereof.

SEC. 108. ACCOUNTING STANDARDS.

(a) AMENDMENT TO SECURITIES ACT OF 1933.—Section 19 of the Securities Act of 1933 (15 U.S.C. 77s) is amended—

(1) By redesignating subsections (b) and (c) as subsections (c) and (d), respectively; and

(2) By inserting after subsection (a) the following:

"(b) RECOGNITION OF ACCOUNTING STANDARDS.

"(1) IN GENERAL.—In carrying out its authority under subsection (a) and under section 13(b) of the Securities Exchange Act of 1934, the Commission may recognize, as 'generally accepted' for purposes of the securities laws, any accounting principles established by a standard setting body—

"(A) that—

"(i) is organized as a private entity;

"(ii) has, for administrative and operational purposes, a board of trustees (or equivalent body) serving in the public interest, the majority of whom are not, concurrent with their service on such board, and have not been during the 2-year period preceding such service, associated persons of any registered public accounting firm;

"(iii) is funded as provided in section 109 of the Sarbanes-Oxley Act of 2002;

"(iv) has adopted procedures to ensure prompt consideration, by majority vote of its members, of changes to accounting principles necessary to reflect emerging accounting issues and changing business practices; and

"(v) considers, in adopting accounting principles, the need to keep standards current in order to reflect changes in the business environment, the extent to which international convergence on high quality accounting standards is necessary or appropriate in the public interest and for the protection of investors; and

"(B) that the Commission determines has the capacity to assist the Commission in fulfilling the requirements of subsection (a) and section 13(b) of the Securities Exchange Act of 1934, because, at a minimum, the standard setting body is capable of improving the accuracy and effectiveness of financial reporting and the protection of investors under the securities laws.

"(2) ANNUAL REPORT.—A standard setting body described in paragraph (1) shall submit an annual report to the Commission and the public, containing audited financial statements of that standard setting body.".

(b) COMMISSION AUTHORITY.—The Commission shall promulgate such rules and regulations to carry out section 19(b) of the Securities Act of 1933, as added by this section, as it deems necessary or appropriate in the public interest or for the protection of investors.

(c) NO EFFECT ON COMMISSION POWERS.—Nothing in this Act, including this section and the amendment made by this section, shall be construed to impair or limit the authority of the Commission to establish accounting principles or standards for purposes of enforcement of the securities laws.

(d) STUDY AND REPORT ON ADOPTING PRINCIPLES-BASED ACCOUNTING.—
    (1) STUDY.
        (A) IN GENERAL.—The Commission shall conduct a study on the adoption by the United States financial reporting system of a principles-based accounting system.
        (B) STUDY TOPICS.—The study required by subparagraph (A) shall include an examination of—
            (i) The extent to which principles-based accounting and financial reporting exists in the United States;
            (ii) The length of time required for change from a rules-based to a principles-based financial reporting system;
            (iii) The feasibility of and proposed methods by which a principles-based system may be implemented; and
            (iv) A thorough economic analysis of the implementation of a principles-based system.
    (2) REPORT.—Not later than 1 year after the date of enactment of this Act, the Commission shall submit a report on the results of the study required by paragraph (1) to the Committee on Banking, Housing, and Urban Affairs of the Senate and the Committee on Financial Services of the House of Representatives.

SEC. 109. FUNDING.

(a) IN GENERAL.—The Board, and the standard setting body designated pursuant to section 19(b) of the Securities Act of 1933, as amended by section 108, shall be funded as provided in this section.

(b) ANNUAL BUDGETS.—The Board and the standard setting body referred to in subsection (a) shall each establish a budget for each fiscal year, which shall be reviewed and approved according to their respective internal procedures not less than 1 month prior to the commencement of the fiscal year to which the budget pertains (or at the beginning of the Board's first fiscal year, which may be a short fiscal year). The budget of the Board shall be subject to approval by the Commission. The budget for the first fiscal year of the Board shall be prepared and approved promptly following the appointment of the initial five Board members, to permit action by the Board of the organizational tasks contemplated by section 101(d).

(c) SOURCES AND USES OF FUNDS.

(1) RECOVERABLE BUDGET EXPENSES.—The budget of the Board (reduced by any registration or annual fees received under section 102(e) for the year preceding the year for which the budget is being computed), and all of the budget of the standard setting body referred to in subsection (a), for each fiscal year of each of those 2 entities, shall be payable from annual accounting support fees, in accordance with subsections (d) and (e). Accounting support fees and other receipts of the Board and of such standard-setting body shall not be considered public monies of the United States.

(2) FUNDS GENERATED FROM THE COLLECTION OF MONETARY PENALTIES.—Subject to the availability in advance in an appropriations Act, and notwithstanding subsection (i), all funds collected by the Board as a result of the assessment of monetary penalties shall be used to fund a merit scholarship program for undergraduate and graduate students enrolled in accredited accounting degree programs, which program is to be administered by the Board or by an entity or agent identified by the Board.

(d) ANNUAL ACCOUNTING SUPPORT FEE FOR THE BOARD.—

(1) ESTABLISHMENT OF FEE.—The Board shall establish, with the approval of the Commission, a reasonable annual accounting support fee (or a formula for the computation thereof), as may be necessary or appropriate to establish and maintain the Board. Such fee may also cover costs incurred in the Board's first fiscal year (which may be a short fiscal year), or may be levied separately with respect to such short fiscal year.

(2) ASSESSMENTS.—The rules of the Board under paragraph (1) shall provide for the equitable allocation, assessment, and collection by the Board (or an agent appointed by the Board) of the fee established under paragraph (1), among issuers, in accordance with subsection (g), allowing for differentiation among classes of issuers, as appropriate.

(e) ANNUAL ACCOUNTING SUPPORT FEE FOR STANDARD SETTING BODY.

The annual accounting support fee for the standard setting body referred to in subsection (a).

(1) shall be allocated in accordance with subsection (g), and assessed and collected against each issuer, on behalf of the standard setting body, by 1 or more appropriate designated collection agents, as may be necessary or appropriate to pay for the budget and provide for the expenses of that standard setting body, and to provide for an independent, stable source of funding for such body, subject to review by the Commission; and

(2) may differentiate among different classes of issuers.

(f) LIMITATION ON FEE.— The amount of fees collected under this section for a fiscal year on behalf of the Board or the standards setting body, as the case may be, shall not exceed the recoverable budget expenses of the Board or body, respectively (which may include operating, capital, and accrued items), referred to in subsection (c)(1).

(g) ALLOCATION OF ACCOUNTING SUPPORT FEES AMONG ISSUERS.—

Any amount due from issuers (or a particular class of issuers) under this section to fund the budget of the Board or the standard setting body referred to in subsection (a) shall be allocated among and payable by each issuer (or each issuer in a particular class, as applicable) in an amount equal to the total of such amount, multiplied by a fraction:

(1) the numerator of which is the average monthly equity market capitalization of the issuer for the 12-month period immediately preceding the beginning of the fiscal year to which such budget relates; and

(2) the denominator of which is the average monthly equity market capitalization of all such issuers for such 12-month period.

(h) CONFORMING AMENDMENTS.—

Section 13(b) (2) of the Securities Exchange Act of 1934 (15 U.S.C. 78m (b)(2)) is amended—

(1) in subparagraph (A), by striking "and" at the end; and

(2) in subparagraph (B), by striking the period at the end and inserting the following: "; and "(C) notwithstanding any other provision of law, pay the allocable share of such issuer of a reasonable annual accounting support fee or fees, determined in accordance with section 109 of the Sarbanes-Oxley Act of 2002.".

(i) RULE OF CONSTRUCTION.—Nothing in this section shall be construed to render either the Board, the standard setting body referred to in subsection (a), or both, subject to procedures in Congress to authorize or appropriate public funds, or to prevent such organization from utilizing additional sources of revenue for its activities, such as earnings from publication sales, provided that each additional source of revenue shall not jeopardize, in the judgment of the Commission, the actual and perceived independence of such organization.

(j) START-UP EXPENSES OF THE BOARD.—From the unexpended balances of the appropriations to the Commission for fiscal year 2003, the Secretary of the Treasury is authorized to advance to the Board not to exceed the amount necessary to cover the expenses of the Board during its first fiscal year (which may be a short fiscal year).

Section 101 – Establishment; Administrative Provisions
Domain: Deterrence
Knowledge Area: Accounting and Finance, Law, Ethics and Compliance
SOX Process: Audit Compliance and Enforcement

Section 101 Synopsis
The Public Company Accounting Oversight Board (PCAOB) is a nonprofit corporation which oversees the audit of public companies, protects the interests of investors, and furthers the public interest with the preparation of informative, accurate, and independent audit reports of companies with securities that are sold to, and held by and for, public investors. Section 101 establishes the authority and responsibilities of a Board to act and support the goals of the PCAOB.

Duties of the PCAOB Board
Primary duties of the PCAOB Board include:
- registering public accounting firms that prepare audit reports for issuers
- establishing or adopting auditing, quality control, ethics, independence and standard practices in the preparation of audit reports
- conducting investigations and disciplinary proceedings of registered accounting firms
- enforcing compliance with the SOX Act
- setting PCAOB budget, and managing Board operations and staff

Board Membership
- composed of Chairperson and four other members
- two members must be, or have been, certified public accountants
- the Chairperson cannot have been a practicing certified public account for at least 5 years
- each member must serve on the board on a full-time basis
- none of the members may be receiving any profits or payments from any public accounting firm, other than retirement payments, or similar types of payments
- PCAOB duration of service are 5 year terms, and no member is allowed more than 2 terms

Powers of the PCAOB consist of the following:
- to sue, be sued, complain, or defend, with the approval of the SEC, in any federal, state or other court
- to operate and maintain offices (lease, buy) in accordance with the powers of the Act in any state
- to appoint employees (accountants, attorneys as appropriate), determine qualifications, define duties, and fix salaries and other compensation, in accordance with the Act
- to enter into operation management agreements, execute obligations, rights and powers imposed or granted by the Board in accordance with the Act

Rules of the Board (Subject to the approval of the SEC):
- provide for the operation and the administration of the board, per the exercise of its authority and responsibilities of the Act

- the Board to delegate, per its internal functions: review of any actions; including hearing, ordering, certifying, and reporting; a person may be entitled to a review by the Board, with respect to any delegated matters or decisions or appeals; if a review is declined or not sought, it will be deemed an action of the Board
- establish ethics, rules and standards of conduct, including a bar on practice for former Board members and non-Board members

Section 101 GASP
- Practitioners must ensure they comply with the statutes of the PCAOB.
- Public accounting firms must register with the PCAOB and abide by the regulatory powers of the body.

Section 102 – Registration with the Board
Domain: Accountability, Transparency, Deterrence
Knowledge Area: Accounting and Finance, Internal and External Audit
SOX Process: Audit and Compliance Enforcement

Section 102 Synopsis
- It is unlawful for any non-registered public accounting firm to prepare or issue an audit report. All unregistered public accounting firms, who wish to audit publicly traded companies, must register with the PCAOB, otherwise they are not legally permitted to prepare or issue audit reports on behalf of public companies.
- Registration applications are assessed by the PCAOB and mandatory, periodic reports are assessed in accordance with PCAOB rulings.
- Mandatory registration and annual fees apply to each public accounting firm registering with the PCAOB.
- Registration applications may only be in the form prescribed by the PCAOB.
- Each application for registration under this subsection shall include consenting compliance:
  - Action of Applications
  - Periodic Reports
  - Public Availability
  - Registration and Annual Fees

- The PCAOB may require more frequent reports, which disclose accounting disagreements between the issuers and the firm in connection with the audit report.

Section 102 GASP
- All public accounting firms, that audit publicly traded companies, must register with the PCAOB, no later than 180 days after the date of the determination of the Commission.
- In preparing annual reports submitted to the PCAOB, the accuracy and currency of information must be the highest priority. If the PCAOB feels the reports are lacking, the Board may request more frequent reports to assist in the disclosure of accounting details and settle disagreements between issuers and the public accounting firms.
- The issuer's audit committee is required to ensure the public accounting firm hired to issue their audit report has been properly registered with the PCAOB.

Section 103 – Auditing, Quality Control, and Independence Standards and Rules
Domain: Governance, Independence
Knowledge Area: Accounting and Finance, Internal and External Audit
SOX Process: Audit and Compliance Enforcement

Section 103 Synopsis
- The PCAOB shall establish the appropriate adoption of standards proposed by professional groups of accountants.
- The PCAOB shall determine appropriate standards for auditing, quality control, and ethics, in accordance with the Sarbanes-Oxley Act.
- The PCAOB closely monitors rule requirements including: the auditing standards of registered public accounting firms, the preparation and statutory retention of reports for 7 years, IT generated reports and adherence to control structures and procedures.
- The PCAOB also closely monitors procedures, professionalism, ethics, and the independence of external audit activities.

Public Accounting Firm Quality Assurance Requirements
- identifies requirements to public accounting firms for their internal quality assurance requirements, documentation and reporting:
  - prepare and maintain audit work papers for 7 years
  - employ second partner review and approval process
- specific auditor attestations related to Section 404 including testing of internal control structures and procedures of the issuer
- maintain records accurately reflecting the transaction and dispositions of assets by the issuer
- provide reasonable assurance that transactions are recorded as necessary to prepare financial statements in accordance with GAAP
- material weaknesses are described in the internal controls relating to any material non-compliance found during the testing of internal controls

Section 103 GASP
- Registered public accounting firms must adhere to the rules determined by the PCAOB regarding auditing, quality control, independence, ethics, rules, and standards.
- Public companies must be aware of the PCAOB requirements, processes, reviews, and recent issues of scrutiny to comply with their auditor's SOX requirements. SOX documentation is a requirement beyond the company's review with their auditors, as auditing firms have their own documentation and review requirements. Companies must provide robust systems for documenting key control activities, as well as establishing appropriate retention mechanisms.
  - Auditor independence, transparency and reporting of any fees or projects outside of the annual audit by the company's audit firm will be reported.
  - Management needs to carefully consider the appearance of conflict of interest when using audit firm's for company projects.

Section 104 – Inspections of Registered Public Accounting Firms
Domain: Deterrence, Independence
Knowledge Area: Accounting and Finance, Internal and External Audit
SOX Process: Audit and Compliance Enforcement

Section 104 Synopsis
- All registered public accounting firms will be subjected to a continuing program of inspections to assess adherence and compliance to PCAOB rules, professional standards, performance of audits, the issue of audit reports, and other matters related to the PCAOB jurisdiction.
- Inspection frequency can vary from 1-3 years, depending on the number of issuers. Adjustments to inspection schedules are permitted, consistent with the purposes of the Act.
- The PCAOB will inspect to the fullest extent of the Act.
- The PCAOB provides a report to the SEC of all inspections, including frequency, procedures and review details. If a registered public accounting firm does not agree with the PCAOB findings they have 30 days to seek a review from the SEC.

Section 104 GASP
- Registered public accounting firms must maintain accurate and current reporting as they can be subjected to inspection. The frequency and timing of the inspections are determined by the number of public companies they audit and considered of appropriate consistency by the PCAOB.
- Registered public accounting firms must retain audit records for 7 years. The PCAOB has the power to inspect documentation in order to determine compliance with this record retention policy. Appropriate record details are subject to report protection and confidentiality determined by the PCAOB.
- When registered public accounting firms disagree with a PCAOB judgement they may seek review from the SEC.

Section 105 – Investigations and Disciplinary Proceedings
Domain: Deterrence
Knowledge Area: Accounting and Finance, Internal and External Audit
SOX Process: Audit and Compliance Enforcement

Section 105 Synopsis
Rules for Investigations and Disciplinary Proceedings
- The PCAOB has established rules and subject requirements for investigations and disciplinary proceedings enacted against public accounting firms. These are exercised, if deemed appropriate, as a result of review findings.
- Registered public accounting firms must provide the PCAOB with all testimony, documentation and audit papers upon request.
- All parties may be subject to subpoena. The PCAOB will notify the SEC of pending investigations and disciplinary proceedings and thereafter will co-ordinate with the SEC Division of Enforcement.
- The PCAOB may refer an investigation to the SEC, other functional regulators; per Gramm-Leach-Bliley Act., Attorneys of one or more states of the US or State Regulatory Authorities.
- The documents used for an investigation (except where directed by the SEC, Attorney General of the US, or other statutory body), are confidential and will not be subject to civil discovery, or disclosure under the Freedom of Information Act.
- Documents used for an investigation may also be made available to government agencies such as the Attorney General or other investigative body, without the loss of privileged or confidential status as appropriate to accomplish the purposes of the Act.
- Employees of the PCAOB undertaking an investigation are subject to immunity protection from civil liability, arising out of an investigation as a federal employee.

Disciplinary Procedures
- In the event that a registered public accounting firm or an associated person should face disciplinary procedures, such procedures will include the following:
    - **Notification and record-keeping**: the PCAOB will bring specific charges, notify the person of the opportunity to defend against such charges and keep a record of proceedings
    - **Public hearings:** proceedings will not be made available to the public, unless determined by the PCAOB with the consent of all the parties

- **Supporting statement**: an official declaration by the PCAOB that a registered public accounting firm or an associated person has been determined by the PCAOB to be part of a sanction

- The following conduct will lead to disciplinary action:
  - **Intentional or other knowing conduct**: includes reckless conduct, violation of professional and regulatory standards, and negligent conduct
  - **Failure to supervise**: when a supervisor is negligent in the execution of his/her duties

- The following sanctions may result from disciplinary action:
  - **Sanction determinations:** require supporting statements; temporary or permanent suspension, barring from practice, and civil money penalties: $100,000 natural person, $2,000,000 for other person; if the penalty covers intentional, knowing or repeated conduct, by a natural person, the fine is: $750,000, or by other person (corporation), the fine is: $15,000,000
  - **Suspended association**: a person who has been suspended may not have a remaining association with a public accounting firm, without the consent of the PCAOB or SEC; it is also unlawful for any person who is suspended or barred to be associated with an issuer in an accountancy or financial capacity without the consent of the PCAOB or SEC
  - **Reporting sanctions:** the PCAOB must report sanctions to the SEC, State regulatory authority and the public; sanction reports contain, name description and other information as appropriate
  - **Stay of sanctions**: a person may have the possible stay of disciplinary action via application to the Commission for review; this may also be exercised after the disciplinary period has ended; hearing may consist solely on a submission of affidavits or presentation of oral arguments that no stay will continue to operate
  - **Expedited procedures**: the SEC has established appropriate cases for expedited procedure for consideration and determination of the duration of a stay pending review of any disciplinary action of the board

Section 105 GASP
- Registered public accounting firms must abide by the PCAOB rules, subject requirements, procedures, professional ethics standards and inspection program to the fullest extent.
- Non-compliance with investigation and disciplinary proceedings, procedures and outcomes, will result in the public accounting firm's suspension or barring from practice and penalties.

Section 106 - Foreign Public Accounting Firms
Domain: Governance
Knowledge Area: Accounting and Finance, Internal and External Audit
SOX Process: Audit and Compliance Enforcement

Section 106 Synopsis
Implications for Foreign Public Accounting Firms
- Foreign accounting firms are subjected to all rules, regulations and standards of the PCAOB.
- Any foreign public accounting firm that prepares an audit report for any issuer of securities publicly traded in the United States, is to be considered by the PCAOB under the same guidelines as a public accounting firm based in the US
- Even if foreign public accounting firms do not issue reports, they may still be considered under the jurisdiction of the PCAOB.
- Depending on the specific circumstance, the SEC and the PCAOB may determine that foreign public firms may also be exempt.

Section 106 GASP
- Foreign public accounting firms must ensure their status with the PCAOB, as to whether they are exempt from requirements of the PCAOB. If they are not exempt, then they must fulfill the same roles as public accounting firms in the US, and can be subjected to the fullest extent of meeting the standards and requirements of the PCAOB.
- Any exemptions from meeting this classification are determined by the PCAOB.

Section 107 – Commission Oversight of the Board
Domain: Governance, Deterrence
Knowledge Area: Accounting and Finance, Internal and External Audit
SOX Process: Audit and Compliance Enforcement

Section 107 Synopsis
SEC Governance
- The SEC has full oversight and enforcement authority over the PCAOB.
- The PCAOB must submit all new or modified rules to the SEC for approval.
- The Securities Exchange Act of 1934 stipulates that the SEC will govern the rules of the PCAOB as if it were a 'registered securities association', consistent with the requirements, rules and regulations of this Title.
- The SEC is responsible, for rule amendment, if it is found that rules are to be deleted, repealed, or modified to more fairly enable the PCAOB to govern.
- The SEC will also review the final sanctions determined by the PCAOB and may enhance, modify, revoke or reduce based on review findings not in keeping with the fairness and appropriateness of the SOX Act.
- The SEC has the power of censure and removal from office PCAOB members who willfully violate any provision of the SOX Act, have willfully abused the authority of being a PCAOB member, or failed to enforce compliance to the SOX Act in keeping with the role of a PCAOB member.

Section 107 GASP
- Public accounting firms must ensure full compliance with the PCAOB rules, regulations, standards, and professional ethics, or else they will be subjected to the scrutiny of the SEC and the statutes of the Securities Exchange Act of 1934.

Section 108 – Accounting Standards
Domain: Governance, Deterrence
Knowledge Area: Accounting and Finance, Internal and External Audit
SOX Process: Audit and Compliance Enforcement

Section 108 Synopsis
Accounting Standards Establishment
- The SEC will recognize 'generally accepted' accounting principles, established by a standard setting body. The standards setting body is to be a private entity and have a board of trustees serving in the public interest. The members of the board will not have practiced for a period of at least 2 years with any registered public accounting firm.
- This standard setting body is funded by the yearly fiscal budget of the SOX Act. The standard setting body is deemed to improve the accuracy and effectiveness of financial reporting and protect investors under the Securities Exchange Act of 1934. The standard setting body's responsibilities include:
  - Compiling an annual report containing audited financial statements study and a report on adopting principle-based accounting (due July 23, 2003 to the committee of Banking, Housing and Urban Affairs of the Senate and the Committee on Financial Services of the House of Representatives). The Report was delivered July 25, 2003. This report also reviews the transition time to move from a rules-based to a principal-based financial reporting system, and an economic analysis of this effort. Reports are available from the SEC on the results of this study. (See References for details.)

Section 108 GASP
- At the planning stages of the organization's Sarbanes-Oxley project, the accounting leadership of the company, namely, the CFO and CFO-nominated Issuers Audit Committee members, should inquire with their outside auditors as to new requirements of the PCAOB or new implementation of those requirements within their firm.
- This discussion should provide the company with insight as to any required or desired modifications in the Sarbanes-Oxley program for the year.

Section 109 – Funding
Domain: Governance
Knowledge Area: Accounting and Finance, Internal and External Audit
SOX Process: Audit and Compliance Enforcement

Section 109 Synopsis
PCAOB Budgetary Practices
- The PCAOB and the standard setting body establish a budget every fiscal year. Budgets are subject to review and approval per internal procedures.
- Budget expenses are payable from annual accounting support fees and will not be considered public monies.
- Funding is supplied via PCAOB assessments, annual accounting support fees for the standard setting body and among issuers or classes of issuers. The amount of fees collected must not exceed recoverable budget expenses from the PCAOB or standards body (including operating, capital or accrued items).
- Funds generated from the collection of penalties, are used to fund a merit scholarship programs for undergraduate and graduate students enrolled in accredited accounting degree programs. This program is operated by the PCAOB or an agent nominated by the PCAOB.

Section 109 GASP
- None Noted.

CHAPTER 2:
Auditor Independence

Practitioners Perspective and Regulation Synopsis

The main focus of this Title is to amend Section 10A, subsections (g) through (l), of the Securities Exchange Act of 1934, which is concerned with auditor and audit committee requirements:

- focuses on conflict of interests stemming from close relationship between audit firms and the companies they audit
- prohibits auditors from performing certain non-audit services
- allows audit committees to pre-approve some activities for non-audit services that are not expressly forbidden by Title II of the SOX Act

Regulation Text

SEC. 201. SERVICES OUTSIDE THE SCOPE OF PRACTICE OF AUDITORS.

(a) PROHIBITED ACTIVITIES- Section 10A of the Securities Exchange Act of 1934 (15 U.S.C. 78j-1) is amended by adding at the end the following:

(g) PROHIBITED ACTIVITIES- Except as provided in subsection (h), it shall be unlawful for a registered public accounting firm (and any associated person of that firm, to the extent determined appropriate by the Commission) that performs for any issuer any audit required by this title or the rules of the Commission under this title or, beginning 180 days after the date of commencement of the operations of the Public Company Accounting Oversight Board established under section 101 of the Sarbanes-Oxley Act of 2002 (in this section referred to as the 'Board'), the rules of the Board, to provide to that issuer, contemporaneously with the audit, any non-audit service, including--

(1) bookkeeping or other services related to the accounting records or financial statements of the audit client;
(2) financial information systems design and implementation;
(3) appraisal or valuation services, fairness opinions, or contribution-in-kind reports;
(4) actuarial services;
(5) internal audit outsourcing services;
(6) management functions or human resources;
(7) broker or dealer, investment adviser, or investment banking services;
(8) legal services and expert services unrelated to the audit; and
(9) any other service that the Board determines, by regulation, is impermissible.

(h) PREAPPROVAL REQUIRED FOR NON-AUDIT SERVICES- A registered public accounting firm may engage in any non-audit service, including tax services, that is, not described in any of paragraphs (1) through (9) of subsection (g) for an audit client, only if the activity is approved in advance by the audit committee of the issuer, in accordance with subsection (i).

(b) EXEMPTION AUTHORITY- The Board may, on a case by case basis, exempt any person, issuer, public accounting firm, or transaction from the prohibition on the provision of services under section 10A(g) of the Securities Exchange Act of 1934 (as added by this section), to the extent that such exemption is necessary or appropriate in the public interest and is consistent with the protection of investors, and subject to review by the Commission in the same manner as for rules of the Board under section 107securities to which section 10A(a) of the Securities Exchange Act of 1934 (15 U.S.C. 78j–1(a)) applies. The Commission may, from time to time, amend or supplement the rules and regulations that it is required to promulgate under this section, after adequate notice and an opportunity for comment, in order to ensure that such rules and regulations adequately comport with the purposes of this section.

(b) Whoever knowingly and willfully violates subsection (a)(1), or any rule or regulation promulgated by the Securities and Exchange Commission under subsection (a)(2), shall be fined under this title, imprisoned not more than 10 years, or both.

(c) Nothing in this section shall be deemed to diminish or relieve any person of any other duty or obligation imposed by Federal or State law or regulation to maintain, or refrain from destroying, any document.

(b) CLERICAL AMENDMENT.—The table of sections at the beginning of chapter 73 of title 18, United States Code, is amended by adding at the end the following new items:

>1519. Destruction, alteration, or falsification of records in Federal investigations and bankruptcy.
>1520. Destruction of corporate audit records.

SEC. 202. PREAPPROVAL REQUIREMENTS.

Section 10A of the Securities Exchange Act of 1934 (15 U.S.C. 78j-1), as amended by this Act, is amended by adding at the end the following:

>(i) PREAPPROVAL REQUIREMENTS-
>>(1) IN GENERAL-
>>>(A) AUDIT COMMITTEE ACTION- All auditing services (which may entail providing comfort letters in connection with securities underwritings or statutory audits required for insurance companies for purposes of State law) and non-audit services, other than as provided in subparagraph (B), provided to an issuer by the auditor of the issuer shall be pre-approved by the audit committee of the issuer.
>>>(B) DE MINIMUS EXCEPTION- The pre-approval requirement under subparagraph (A) is waived with respect to the provision of non-audit services for an issuer, if--
>>>>(i) the aggregate amount of all such non-audit services provided to the issuer constitutes not more than 5 percent of the total amount of revenues paid by the issuer to its auditor during the fiscal year in which the non-audit services are provided;
>>>>(ii) such services were not recognized by the issuer at the time of the engagement to be non-audit services; and
>>>>(iii) such services are promptly brought to the attention of the audit committee of the issuer and approved prior to the completion of the audit by the audit committee or by 1 or more members of the audit committee who are members of the board of directors to whom authority to grant such approvals has been delegated by the audit committee.

(2) DISCLOSURE TO INVESTORS- Approval by an audit committee of an issuer under this subsection of a non-audit service to be performed by the auditor of the issuer shall be disclosed to investors in periodic reports required by section 13(a).

(3) DELEGATION AUTHORITY- The audit committee of an issuer may delegate to 1 or more designated members of the audit committee who are independent directors of the board of directors, the authority to grant pre-approvals required by this subsection. The decisions of any member to whom authority is delegated under this paragraph to pre-approve an activity under this subsection shall be presented to the full audit committee at each of its scheduled meetings.

(4) APPROVAL OF AUDIT SERVICES FOR OTHER PURPOSES- In carrying out its duties under subsection (m)(2), if the audit committee of an issuer approves an audit service within the scope of the engagement of the auditor, such audit service shall be deemed to have been pre-approved for purposes of this subsection.'

SEC. 203. AUDIT PARTNER ROTATION.

Section 10A of the Securities Exchange Act of 1934 (15 U.S.C. 78j-1), as amended by this Act, is amended by adding at the end the following:

(j) AUDIT PARTNER ROTATION- It shall be unlawful for a registered public accounting firm to provide audit services to an issuer if the lead (or co-ordinating) audit partner (having primary responsibility for the audit), or the audit partner responsible for reviewing the audit, has performed audit services for that issuer in each of the 5 previous fiscal years of that issuer.'

SEC. 204. AUDITOR REPORTS TO AUDIT COMMITTEES.

Section 10A of the Securities Exchange Act of 1934 (15 U.S.C. 78j-1), as amended by this Act, is amended by adding at the end the following:

(k) REPORTS TO AUDIT COMMITTEES- Each registered public accounting firm that performs for any issuer any audit required by this title shall timely report to the audit committee of the issuer--

(1) all critical accounting policies and practices to be used;

(2) all alternative treatments of financial information within generally accepted accounting principles that have been discussed with management officials of the issuer, ramifications of the use of such alternative disclosures and treatments, and the treatment preferred by the registered public accounting firm; and

(3) other material written communications between the registered public accounting firm and the management of the issuer, such as any management letter or schedule of unadjusted differences.

SEC.205. CONFORMING AMENDMENTS.

(a) DEFINITIONS- Section 3(a) of the Securities Exchange Act of 1934 (15 U.S.C. 78c(a)) is amended by adding at the end the following:

(58) AUDIT COMMITTEE- The term `audit committee' means--

(A) a committee (or equivalent body) established by and amongst the board of directors of an issuer for the purpose of overseeing the accounting and financial reporting processes of the issuer and audits of the financial statements of the issuer; and

(B) if no such committee exists with respect to an issuer, the entire board of directors of the issuer.

(59) REGISTERED PUBLIC ACCOUNTING FIRM- The term `registered public accounting firm' has the same meaning as in section 2 of the Sarbanes-Oxley Act of 2002.'

(b) AUDITOR REQUIREMENTS- Section 10A of the Securities Exchange Act of 1934 (15 U.S.C. 78j-1) is amended--

(1) by striking `an independent public accountant' each place that term appears and inserting `a registered public accounting firm';

(2) by striking `the independent public accountant' each place that term appears and inserting `the registered public accounting firm';

(3) in subsection (c), by striking `No independent public accountant' and inserting `No registered public accounting firm'; and

(4) in subsection (b)--

(A) by striking `the accountant' each place that term appears and inserting `the firm';

(B) by striking `such accountant' each place that term appears and inserting `such firm'; and

(C) in paragraph (4), by striking `the accountant's report' and inserting `the report of the firm'.

(c) OTHER REFERENCES- The Securities Exchange Act of 1934 (15 U.S.C. 78a et seq.) is amended--

(1) in section 12(b)(1) (15 U.S.C. 78l(b)(1)), by striking `independent public accountants' each place that term appears and inserting `a registered public accounting firm'; and

(2) in subsections (e) and (i) of section 17 (15 U.S.C. 78q), by striking an independent public accountant' each place that term appears and inserting `a registered public accounting firm'.

(d) CONFORMING AMENDMENT- Section 10A(f) of the Securities Exchange Act of 1934 (15 U.S.C. 78k(f)) is amended--

(1) by striking `DEFINITION' and inserting `DEFINITIONS'; and

(2) by adding at the end the following: `As used in this section, the term issuer' means an issuer (as defined in section 3), the securities of which are registered under section 12, or that is required to file reports pursuant to section 15(d), or that files or has filed a registration statement that has not yet become effective under the Securities Act of 1933 (15 U.S.C. 77a et seq.), and that it has not withdrawn.'.

SEC. 206. CONFLICTS OF INTEREST.

Section 10A of the Securities Exchange Act of 1934 (15 U.S.C. 78j-1), as amended by this Act, is amended by adding at the end the following:

(l) CONFLICTS OF INTEREST- It shall be unlawful for a registered public accounting firm to perform for an issuer any audit service required by this title, if a chief executive officer, controller, chief financial officer, chief accounting officer, or any person serving in an equivalent position for the issuer, was employed by that registered independent public accounting firm and participated in any capacity in the audit of that issuer during the 1-year period preceding the date of the initiation of the audit.'

SEC.207. STUDY OF MANDATORY ROTATION OF REGISTERED PUBLIC ACCOUNTING FIRMS.

(a) STUDY AND REVIEW REQUIRED- The Comptroller General of the United States shall conduct a study and review of the potential effects of requiring the mandatory rotation of registered public accounting firms.

(b) REPORT REQUIRED- Not later than 1 year after the date of enactment of this Act, the Comptroller General shall submit a report to the Committee on Banking, Housing, and Urban Affairs of the Senate and the Committee on Financial Services of the House of Representatives on the results of the study and review required by this section.

(c) DEFINITION- For purposes of this section, the term 'mandatory rotation' refers to the imposition of a limit on the period of years in which a particular registered public accounting firm may be the auditor of record for a particular issuer.

SEC. 208. COMMISSION AUTHORITY.

(a) COMMISSION REGULATIONS- Not later than 180 days after the date of enactment of this Act, the Commission shall issue final regulations to carry out each of subsections (g) through (l) of section 10A of the Securities Exchange Act of 1934, as added by this title.

(b) AUDITOR INDEPENDENCE- It shall be unlawful for any registered public accounting firm (or an associated person thereof, as applicable) to prepare or issue any audit report with respect to any issuer, if the firm or associated person engages in any activity with respect to that issuer prohibited by any of subsections (g) through (l) of section 10A of the Securities Exchange Act of 1934, as added by this title, or any rule or regulation of the Commission or of the Board issued there-under.

SEC. 209. CONSIDERATIONS BY APPROPRIATE STATE REGULATORY AUTHORITIES.

In supervising non-registered public accounting firms and their associated persons, appropriate State regulatory authorities should make an independent determination of the proper standards applicable, particularly taking into consideration the size and nature of the business of the accounting firms they supervise and the size and nature of the business of the clients of those firms. The standards applied by the Board under this Act should not be presumed to be applicable for purposes of this section for small and medium sized non-registered public accounting firms.

Section 201 – Services Outside the Scope of Practice of Auditors
Domain: Independence
Knowledge Area: Internal and External Audit
SOX Process: Planning; Regulations for Others

Section 201 Synopsis
PROHIBITED ACTIVITIES
Unless exempted by the PCAOB, it is against the law for a registered public auditing firm (or associated person) to perform auditing work for an issuer while performing one or more of the following services for the issuer:
- bookkeeping or other services related to the accounting records or financial statements of the audit client
- financial information systems design and implementation
- appraisal or valuation services, fairness opinions, or contribution-in-kind reports
- actuarial services
- internal audit outsourcing services
- management functions or human resources
- broker or dealer, investment adviser, or investment banking services
- legal services and expert services unrelated to the audit
- any other service that the PCAOB determines, by regulation, is impermissible

Exemptions to this rule can be granted on a case-by-case basis by the PCAOB, and subject to SEC review, in the following cases:
- necessary or appropriate in the public interest and is consistent with the protection of investors
- subject to audit review by the Commission, ensuring
  - (a) procedures provide assurance of detecting illegal acts that materially affect financial statements
  - (b) procedures identify third party transactions that materially affect financial statements
  - (c) an evaluation is made as to the issuer's ability to continue during the ensuing fiscal year
  - for example, tax return preparation would be an exempt activity, whereas tax consulting would not be permissible

PREAPPROVAL REQUIRED FOR NON-AUDIT SERVICES

A registered public auditing firm (or associated person) is allowed to perform both auditing work and additional services under certain conditions:

- The additional work must be something other than the prohibited services listed above.
- The work must be pre-approved by the issuer's audit committee.

Issuers who willfully and knowingly violate these rules and regulations can be:

- fined
- imprisoned for up to 10 years
- both fined and imprisoned for up to 10 years

Section 201 GASP
PROHIBITED ACTIVITIES

- Accounting must keep current with PCAOB regulations and identify if any additional non-audit services are prohibited for registered public auditing firms (or associated persons) to be provided while conducting an audit for the issuer.

PREAPPROVAL REQUIRED FOR NON-AUDIT SERVICES

- Department managers for Accounting, Human Resources, Investment, Actuarial, and Legal Services must consult with, and gain written approval from, the audit committee prior to contracting services with a registered public accounting firm (or associated person).
- Before any services are performed by a registered public accounting firm, or person associated with such firm, the audit committee must review and approve (ie pre-approve) the services in writing.

Section 202 – Pre-Approval Requirements

Domain: Governance; Independence
Knowledge Area: Law, Ethics and Compliance; Internal and External Audit
SOX Process: Planning; Regulations for Others

Section 202 Synopsis

All auditing activities provided by a registered public accounting firm (or associated person), must be pre-approved by the audit committee.

All non-audit activities provided by a registered public accounting firm (or associated person), must be pre-approved by the audit committee, except where:
- the aggregate cost of all such non-audit activities is less than 5% of revenues paid to the auditor during the same year
- the services were not recognized as non-audit at the time of engagement
- the services are approved by one or more members of the audit committee before the audit is completed

An audit service shall be deemed to have been pre-approved if the audit committee approves an audit service within the scope of the audit engagement and during the course of its regular duties of appointing, compensating, and overseeing the work of registered public accounting firms employed by that issuer.

Pre-approvals performed by the audit committee must be disclosed in the issuer's annual and quarterly publicly issued financial reports.

The audit committee delegate authority to grant pre-approvals to one or more designated members of the audit committee, with the following requirements:
- designees must be independent directors of the board of directors
- pre-approval decisions must be presented to the full audit committee at each of its scheduled meetings

Section 202 GASP

The audit committee is responsible for evaluating each audit and non-audit service to determine whether it must be pre-approved.

Although it is allowable for the audit committee to appoint and authorize one member of the committee to grant pre-approvals, they should require two or more approvers to avoid potential conflicts of interest.

The audit committee is responsible for appointing, compensating and overseeing the work performed by registered public accounting firms employed by the issuer.
The audit committee, along with Accounting, must disclose all pre-approvals to the public on the quarterly and annual reports to the SEC.

Section 203 – Audit Partner Rotation

Domain: Governance; Independence
Knowledge Area: Law, Ethics and Compliance; Internal and External Audit
SOX Process: Planning; Regulations for Others

Section 203 Synopsis

The same lead audit partner and reviewing partner cannot have primary responsibility for an issuer's audit for more than 5 years in a row.

Section 203 GASP

The audit committee must ensure that a new lead audit partner and reviewing partner are put in charge of the issuer's audit every sixth fiscal year, at a minimum.

Section 204 – Auditor Reports to Audit Committees

Domain: Governance; Independence
Knowledge Area: Law, Ethics and Compliance; Internal and External Audit
SOX Process: Planning; Regulations for Others

Section 204 Synopsis

Registered public accounting firms that perform audits related to the SOX Act must provide timely reports to the issuer's audit committee, including:
- all critical accounting policies and practices to be used
- disclosure and analysis of issuer's alternative accounting methods within GAAP, as revealed by issuer management, which discusses:
  - description of alternate accounting practices, which are compliant with generally accepted accounting principles, that have been discussed with officers and directors of the issuer
  - possible outcome(s) of using the alternative accounting method(s)
  - registered public auditing firm's recommended accounting methods
- written communications between the audit firm and issuer management

Section 204 GASP

The audit committee should meet with audit firm(s) regularly to ensure they receive the following reports and updates timely:
- all critical accounting policies and practices to be used
- disclosure and analysis of issuer's alternative accounting methods within GAAP, as revealed by issuer management, which discusses:

- description of alternate accounting practices, which are compliant with generally accepted accounting principles, that have been discussed with officers and directors of the issuer
- possible outcome(s) of using the alternative accounting method(s)
- registered public auditing firm's recommended accounting methods

The audit committee should evaluate reports, correspondence, analysis and recommendations received from audit firms and plan appropriate follow-up actions with issuer's officers and directors.

Section 205 – Conforming Amendments
Domain: Governance; Independence
Knowledge Area: Law, Ethics and Compliance
SOX Process: Planning; Regulations for Others

Section 205 Synopsis
The audit committee is expected to:
- oversee the accounting and financial reporting processes of the issuer
- oversee audits of the financial statements of the issuer
- be a committee (or equivalent body)
- be established by the board of directors of an issuer
- be comprised of members of the board of directors of an issuer
- if no such committee exists with respect to an issuer, the entire board of directors of the issuer comprises the audit committee

A registered public accounting firm is defined in Section 2 as:
- a proprietorship, partnership, incorporated association, corporation, limited liability company, limited liability partnership, or other legal entity that is engaged in the practice of public accounting or preparing or issuing audit reports
- registered with the Board in accordance with this Act (See Section 102.)

The term 'issuer' is modified in this section. The full definition, including the modification, appears below:
- any person who issues or proposes to issue any security, the securities of which are registered with the SEC by a member, broker or dealer, allowing them to effect any security transaction on a national securities exchange

- the person or persons performing the acts and assuming the duties of depositor or manager pursuant to the provisions of the trust or other agreement or instrument under which such securities are issued, the securities of which are registered with the SEC by a member, broker or dealer, allowing them to effect any security transaction on a national securities exchange, with respect to:
    - certificates of deposit for securities
    - voting-trust certificates
    - collateral-trust certificates
    - certificates of interest not having a board of directors or of the fixed, restricted management, or unit type
    - shares in an unincorporated investment trust not having a board of directors or of the fixed, restricted management, or unit type
- the person by whom the equipment or property is, or is to be, used, the securities of which are registered with the SEC by a member, broker or dealer, allowing them to effect any security transaction on a national securities exchange, with respect to equipment-trust certificates or like securities
- the securities of which are registered with the SEC by a member, broker or dealer, allowing them to effect any security transaction on a national securities exchange
- an issuer who files, or is required to file annual and/or quarterly reports as prescribed by the SEC, and either:
    - filed a registration statement or became operative prior to the enactment date of the Securities Acts Amendments of 1964, or
    - that files or has filed a registration statement that has not yet become effective under the Securities Act of 1933 (15 U.S.C. 77a et seq.), and that it has not withdrawn

Section 205 GASP

The board of directors must select members and/or participate in the audit committee, which will be responsible for the financial reporting process and financial statement audits.

Qualified members of the board of directors should serve on the audit committee with rotating memberships.

Audit committee members should possess knowledge of GAAP, Financial Reporting, Auditing and SOX.

Section 206 – Conflicts of Interest
Domain: Governance; Independence
Knowledge Area: Law, Ethics and Compliance
SOX Process: Planning; Regulations for Others

Section 206 Synopsis
An individual who has provided an audit service to an issuer within the past year cannot be hired as, or serve as, an officer or director of that company.

Section 206 GASP
Human Resources management should ensure that interview candidates for officer and director positions have not been employed by the independent public accounting firm which had provided audit services to the company within the past year.

Section 207 – Study of Mandatory Rotation of Registered Public Accounting Firms
Domain: Governance
Knowledge Area: Law, Ethics and Compliance; Internal and External Audit
SOX Process: Planning; Regulations for Others

Section 207 Synopsis
The Comptroller General of the United States is required to issue a study which reviews the potential effects of the mandatory rotation of auditors.
- The report was issued November 2003 and is available to the public.
- The report findings were inconclusive on whether auditor rotation was an effective way to assure quality and auditor independence. A long-term study was recommended.
- Mandatory rotation' refers to the imposition of a limit on the period of years in which a particular registered public accounting firm may be the auditor of record for a particular issuer. Currently, the mandatory audit partner rotation is set at 5 years, according to the Security Exchange Act of 1934 section 10A subsection (j).

Section 207 GASP
The audit committee should keep up-to-date with mandatory rotation standards and ensure the registered public accounting firms conduct their audits in compliance with the mandate.[1]

Section 208 – Commission Authority
Domain: Governance
Knowledge Area: Law, Ethics and Compliance
SOX Process: Planning; Regulations for Others

Section 208 Synopsis
As amended by Sections 201 through 206 of the Act, the SEC has issued final regulations for carrying out the Securities Exchange Act of 1934 section 10A subsections (g) through (l). The regulations cover the Title 2 amendments in detail, including:
- discussion surrounding conflicts of interest
- detailed descriptions of the services prohibited for registered public accounting firms that are providing audit services for the issuer
- partner rotation rules, including exceptions
- audit committee responsibilities
- disclosure requirements and instructions for completing disclosure forms

In order to maintain auditor independence, a registered public accounting firm cannot issue an audit report if they engage in activities that are prohibited by the Securities Exchange Act of 1934 section 10A subsections (g) through (l), as amended by Sections 201 through 206 of the Act (as summarized above).

Section 208 GASP
- Accounting management must become familiar with SEC regulations developed to comply with section 208. At the time of this writing, final SEC regulations and associated corrections are available via the internet.[2]

---

[1] Contributors: Jeanette M. Franzel, John J. Reilly, Jr., William E. Boutboul, Cheryl E. Clark, Robert W. Gramling, Wilfred B. Holloway, Michael C. Hrapsky, Catherine M. Hurley, Charles E. Norfleet, Judy K. Pagano, Sidney H. Schwartz, Jason O. Strange, Patricia A. Summers, and Walter K. Vance (2003). *PUBLIC ACCOUNTING FIRMS Required Study on the Potential Effects of Mandatory Audit Firm Rotation*. Retrieved August 3, 2007, from the United States General Accounting Office website: http://www.gao.gov/new.items/d04216.pdf

[2] The Securities and Exchange Commission (2003). 17 CFR PARTS 210, 240, 249 and 274 [RELEASE NO. 33-8183; 34-47265; 35-27642; IC-25915; IA-2103, FR-68, File No. S7-49-02] RIN 3235-AI73 Strengthening the Commission's Requirements Regarding Auditor Independence. Retrieved August 6, 2007, from the Securities and Exchange Commission website: http://www.sec.gov/rules/final/33-8183.htm

- Before pre-approving services provided by a registered public accounting firm, the audit committee should investigate the firm's background to make sure they have not engaged in any of the activities prohibited by the Securities Exchange Act of 1934 section 10A subsections (g) through (l), as amended by Sections 201 through 206 of the Act.

Section 209 – Considerations by Appropriate State Regulatory Authorities

Domain: Governance
Knowledge Area: Law, Ethics and Compliance; Internal and External Audit
SOX Process: Regulations for Others

Section 209 Synopsis

The requirements outlined by Title II may not be appropriate or applicable for all accounting firms. State regulatory authorities that supervise the firm should determine the appropriate requirements, depending on the size and nature of the business.

Section 209 GASP

Audit committees should be aware of the requirements that their accounting firms must comply with as determined by state regulatory authorities. Individualized regulations may affect how auditors are appointed, managed, and compensated.

CHAPTER 3:
Corporate Responsibility

Practitioners Perspective and Regulation Synopsis

This Title addresses issues related to Corporate Responsibility. In all areas of internal controls there are specific statements for making internal controls, CEO and CFO sponsored, while operating under a framework that supports them. The ongoing communication between the Audit Committee, the company's Directors and Officers, Public Accounting Firm, employees and beneficiaries is essential for compliance.

Title III includes considerations to employ project over-sight, apply metrics, and improve testing results.

Projects that execute process controls and improvements need to be taken on each quarter to ensure the statements are supported by documentation.

Regulation Text

SEC. 301. PUBLIC COMPANY AUDIT COMMITTEES.
Section 10A of the Securities Exchange Act of 1934 (15 U.S.C. 78f) is amended by adding at the end the following:
(m) STANDARDS RELATING TO AUDIT COMMITTEES.—
    (1) COMMISSION RULES.— H. R. 3763—32
        (A) IN GENERAL.—Effective not later than 270 days after the date of enactment of this subsection, the Commission shall, by rule, direct the national securities exchanges and national securities associations to prohibit the listing of any security of an issuer that is not in compliance with the requirements of any portion of paragraphs (2) through (6).

(B) OPPORTUNITY TO CURE DEFECTS.—The rules of the Commission under subparagraph (A) shall provide for appropriate procedures for an issuer to have an opportunity to cure any defects that would be the basis for a prohibition under subparagraph (A), before the imposition of such prohibition.

(2) RESPONSIBILITIES RELATING TO REGISTERED PUBLIC ACCOUNTING FIRMS.—The audit committee of each issuer, in its capacity as a committee of the board of directors, shall be directly responsible for the appointment, compensation, and oversight of the work of any registered public accounting firm employed by that issuer (including resolution of disagreements between management and the auditor regarding financial reporting) for the purpose of preparing or issuing an audit report or related work, and each such registered public accounting firm shall report directly to the audit committee.

(3) INDEPENDENCE.—

(A) IN GENERAL.—Each member of the audit committee of the issuer shall be a member of the board of directors of the issuer, and shall otherwise be independent.

(B) CRITERIA.—In order to be considered to be independent for purposes of this paragraph, a member of an audit committee of an issuer may not, other than in his or her capacity as a member of the audit committee, the board of directors, or any other board committee—

(i) accept any consulting, advisory, or other compensatory fee from the issuer; or

(ii) be an affiliated person of the issuer or any subsidiary thereof.

(C) EXEMPTION AUTHORITY.—The Commission may exempt from the requirements of subparagraph (B) a particular relationship with respect to audit committee members, as the Commission determines appropriate in light of the circumstances.

(4) COMPLAINTS.—Each audit committee shall establish procedures for—

(A) the receipt, retention, and treatment of complaints received by the issuer regarding accounting, internal accounting controls, or auditing matters; and

(B) the confidential, anonymous submission by employees of the issuer of concerns regarding questionable accounting or auditing matters.

(5) AUTHORITY TO ENGAGE ADVISERS.—Each audit committee shall have the authority to engage independent counsel and other advisers, as it determines necessary to carry out its duties.

(6) FUNDING.—Each issuer shall provide for appropriate funding, as determined by the audit committee, in its capacity as a committee of the board of directors, for payment of compensation— H. R. 3763—33

(A) to the registered public accounting firm employed by the issuer for the purpose of rendering or issuing an audit report; and

(B) to any advisers employed by the audit committee under paragraph (5).

SEC. 302. CORPORATE RESPONSIBILITY FOR FINANCIAL REPORTS.

(a) REGULATIONS REQUIRED.—The Commission shall, by rule, require, for each company filing periodic reports under section 13(a) or 15(d) of the Securities Exchange Act of 1934 (15 U.S.C. 78m, 78o(d)), that the principal executive officer or officers and the principal financial officer or officers, or persons performing similar functions, certify in each annual or quarterly report filed or submitted under either such section of such Act that—

(1) the signing officer has reviewed the report;

(2) based on the officer's knowledge, the report does not contain any untrue statement of a material fact or omit to state a material fact necessary in order to make the statements made, in light of the circumstances under which such statements were made, not misleading;

(3) based on such officer's knowledge, the financial statements, and other financial information included in the report, fairly present in all material respects the financial condition and results of operations of the issuer as of, and for, the periods presented in the report;

(4) the signing officers—

(A) are responsible for establishing and maintaining internal controls;

(B) have designed such internal controls to ensure that material information relating to the issuer and its consolidated subsidiaries is made known to such officers by others within those entities, particularly during the period in which the periodic reports are being prepared;

(C) have evaluated the effectiveness of the issuer's internal controls as of a date within 90 days prior to the report; and

(D) have presented in the report their conclusions about the effectiveness of their internal controls based on their evaluation as of that date;

(5) the signing officers have disclosed to the issuer's auditors and the audit committee of the board of directors (or persons fulfilling the equivalent function)—

(A) all significant deficiencies in the design or operation of internal controls which could adversely affect the issuer's ability to record, process, summarize, and report financial data and have identified for the issuer's auditors any material weaknesses in internal controls; and

(B) any fraud, whether or not material, that involves management or other employees who have a significant role in the issuer's internal controls; and

(6) the signing officers have indicated in the report whether or not there were significant changes in internal controls or in other factors that could significantly affect internal controls subsequent to the date of their evaluation, including any corrective actions with regard to significant deficiencies and material weaknesses. H. R. 3763—34

(b) FOREIGN REINCORPORATIONS HAVE NO EFFECT.—Nothing in this section 302 shall be interpreted or applied in any way to allow any issuer to lessen the legal force of the statement required under this section 302, by an issuer having reincorporated or having engaged in any other transaction that resulted in the transfer of the corporate domicile or offices of the issuer from inside the United States to outside of the United States.

(c) DEADLINE.—The rules required by subsection (a) shall be effective not later than 30 days after the date of enactment of this Act.

SEC. 303. IMPROPER INFLUENCE ON CONDUCT OF AUDITS.

(a) RULES TO PROHIBIT.—It shall be unlawful, in contravention of such rules or regulations as the Commission shall prescribe as necessary and appropriate in the public interest or for the protection of investors, for any officer or director of an issuer, or any other person acting under the direction thereof, to take any action to fraudulently influence, coerce, manipulate, or mislead any independent public or certified accountant engaged in the performance of an audit of the financial statements of that issuer for the purpose of rendering such financial statements materially misleading.

(b) ENFORCEMENT.—In any civil proceeding, the Commission shall have exclusive authority to enforce this section and any rule or regulation issued under this section.

(c) NO PREEMPTION OF OTHER LAW.—The provisions of subsection (a) shall be in addition to, and shall not supersede or preempt, any other provision of law or any rule or regulation issued thereunder.

(d) DEADLINE FOR RULEMAKING.—The Commission shall—
    (1) propose the rules or regulations required by this section, not later than 90 days after the date of enactment of this Act; and
    (2) issue final rules or regulations required by this section, not later than 270 days after that date of enactment.

SEC. 304. FORFEITURE OF CERTAIN BONUSES AND PROFITS.

(a) ADDITIONAL COMPENSATION PRIOR TO NONCOMPLIANCE WITH COMMISSION FINANCIAL REPORTING REQUIREMENTS.—If an issuer is required to prepare an accounting restatement due to the material noncompliance of the issuer, as a result of misconduct, with any financial reporting requirement under the securities laws, the chief executive officer and chief financial officer of the issuer shall reimburse the issuer for—
    (1) any bonus or other incentive-based or equity-based compensation received by that person from the issuer during the 12-month period following the first public issuance or filing with the Commission (whichever first occurs) of the financial document embodying such financial reporting requirement; and
    (2) any profits realized from the sale of securities of the issuer during that 12-month period.

(b) COMMISSION EXEMPTION AUTHORITY.—The Commission may exempt any person from the application of subsection (a), as it deems necessary and appropriate.

SEC. 305. OFFICER AND DIRECTOR BARS AND PENALTIES.

(a) UNFITNESS STANDARD.—

H. R. 3763—35

(1) SECURITIES EXCHANGE ACT OF 1934.—Section 21(d)(2) of the Securities Exchange Act of 1934 (15 U.S.C. 78u(d)(2)) is amended by striking "substantial unfitness" and inserting "unfitness".

(2) SECURITIES ACT OF 1933.—Section 20(e) of the Securities Act of 1933 (15 U.S.C. 77t(e)) is amended by striking "substantial unfitness" and inserting "unfitness".

(b) EQUITABLE RELIEF.—Section 21(d) of the Securities Exchange Act of 1934 (15 U.S.C. 78u(d)) is amended by adding at the end the following:

"(5) EQUITABLE RELIEF.—In any action or proceeding brought or instituted by the Commission under any provision of the securities laws, the Commission may seek, and any Federal court may grant, any equitable relief that may be appropriate or necessary for the benefit of investors.".

SEC. 306. INSIDER TRADES DURING PENSION FUND BLACKOUT PERIODS.

(a) PROHIBITION OF INSIDER TRADING DURING PENSION FUND BLACKOUT PERIODS.—

(1) IN GENERAL.—Except to the extent otherwise provided by rule of the Commission pursuant to paragraph (3), it shall be unlawful for any director or executive officer of an issuer of any equity security (other than an exempted security), directly or indirectly, to purchase, sell, or otherwise acquire or transfer any equity security of the issuer (other than an exempted security) during any blackout period with respect to such equity security if such director or officer acquires such equity security in connection with his or her service or employment as a director or executive officer.

(2) REMEDY.—

(A) IN GENERAL.—Any profit realized by a director or executive officer referred to in paragraph (1) from any purchase, sale, or other acquisition or transfer in violation of this subsection shall inure to and be recoverable by the issuer, irrespective of any intention on the part of such director or executive officer in entering into the transaction.

(B) ACTIONS TO RECOVER PROFITS.—An action to recover profits in accordance with this subsection may be instituted at law or in equity in any court of competent jurisdiction by the issuer, or by the owner of any security of the issuer in the name and in behalf of the issuer if the issuer fails or refuses to bring such action within 60 days after the date of request, or fails diligently to prosecute the action thereafter, except that no such suit shall be brought more than 2 years after the date on which such profit was realized.

(3) RULEMAKING AUTHORIZED.—The Commission shall, in consultation with the Secretary of Labor, issue rules to clarify the application of this subsection and to prevent evasion thereof. Such rules shall provide for the application of the requirements of paragraph (1) with respect to entities treated as a single employer with respect to an issuer under section 414(b), (c), (m), or (o) of the Internal Revenue Code of 1986 to the extent necessary to clarify the application of such requirements and to prevent evasion thereof. Such rules may also provide for H. R. 3763—36 appropriate exceptions from the requirements of this subsection, including exceptions for purchases pursuant to an automatic dividend reinvestment program or purchases or sales made pursuant to an advance election.

(4) BLACKOUT PERIOD.—For purposes of this subsection, the term "blackout period", with respect to the equity securities of any issuer—

(A) means any period of more than 3 consecutive business days during which the ability of not fewer than 50 percent of the participants or beneficiaries under all individual account plans maintained by the issuer to purchase, sell, or otherwise acquire or transfer an interest in any equity of such issuer held in such an individual account plan is temporarily suspended by the issuer or by a fiduciary of the plan; and

(B) does not include, under regulations which shall be prescribed by the Commission—

(i) a regularly scheduled period in which the participants and beneficiaries may not purchase, sell, or otherwise acquire or transfer an interest in any equity of such issuer, if such period is—

(I) incorporated into the individual account plan; and (II) timely disclosed to employees before becoming participants under the individual account plan or as a subsequent amendment to the plan; or

(ii) any suspension described in subparagraph (A) that is imposed solely in connection with persons becoming participants or beneficiaries, or ceasing to be participants or beneficiaries, in an individual account plan by reason of a corporate merger, acquisition, divestiture, or similar transaction involving the plan or plan sponsor.

(5) INDIVIDUAL ACCOUNT PLAN.—For purposes of this subsection, the term "individual account plan" has the meaning provided in section 3(34) of the Employee Retirement Income Security Act of 1974 (29 U.S.C. 1002(34), except that such term shall not include a one-participant retirement plan (within the meaning of section 101(i)(8)(B) of such Act (29 U.S.C. 1021(i)(8)(B))).

(6) NOTICE TO DIRECTORS, EXECUTIVE OFFICERS, AND THE COMMISSION.—In any case in which a director or executive officer is subject to the requirements of this subsection in connection with a blackout period (as defined in paragraph (4)) with respect to any equity securities, the issuer of such equity securities shall timely notify such director or officer and the Securities and Exchange Commission of such blackout period.

(b) NOTICE REQUIREMENTS TO PARTICIPANTS AND BENEFICIARIES UNDER ERISA.—

(1) IN GENERAL.—Section 101 of the Employee Retirement Income Security Act of 1974 (29 U.S.C. 1021) is amended by redesignating the second subsection (h) as subsection (j), and by inserting after the first subsection (h) the following new subsection:

H. R. 3763—37 "(i) NOTICE OF BLACKOUT PERIODS TO PARTICIPANT OR BENEFICIARY UNDER INDIVIDUAL ACCOUNT PLAN.—

"(1) DUTIES OF PLAN ADMINISTRATOR.—In advance of the commencement of any blackout period with respect to an individual account plan, the plan administrator shall notify the plan participants and beneficiaries who are affected by such action in accordance with this subsection.

"(2) NOTICE REQUIREMENTS.—

"(A) IN GENERAL.—The notices described in paragraph (1) shall be written in a manner calculated to be understood by the average plan participant and shall include—

"(i) the reasons for the blackout period,

"(ii) an identification of the investments and other rights affected,

"(iii) the expected beginning date and length of the blackout period,

"(iv) in the case of investments affected, a statement that the participant or beneficiary should evaluate the appropriateness of their current investment decisions in light of their inability to direct or diversify assets credited to their accounts during the blackout period, and

"(v) such other matters as the Secretary may require by regulation.

"(B) NOTICE TO PARTICIPANTS AND BENEFICIARIES.—Except as otherwise provided in this subsection, notices described in paragraph (1) shall be furnished to all participants and beneficiaries under the plan to whom the blackout period applies at least 30 days in advance of the blackout period.

"(C) EXCEPTION TO 30-DAY NOTICE REQUIREMENT.—In any case in which—

"(i) a deferral of the blackout period would violate the requirements of subparagraph (A) or (B) of section 404(a)(1), and a fiduciary of the plan reasonably so determines in writing, or "(ii) the inability to provide the 30-day advance notice is due to events that were unforeseeable or circumstances beyond the reasonable control of the plan administrator, and a fiduciary of the plan reasonably so determines in writing, subparagraph (B) shall not apply, and the notice shall be furnished to all participants and beneficiaries under the plan to whom the blackout period applies as soon as reasonably possible under the circumstances unless such a notice in advance of the termination of the blackout period is impracticable.

"(D) WRITTEN NOTICE.—The notice required to be provided under this subsection shall be in writing, except that such notice may be in electronic or other form to the extent that such form is reasonably accessible to the recipient.

"(E) NOTICE TO ISSUERS OF EMPLOYER SECURITIES SUBJECT TO BLACKOUT PERIOD.—In the case of any blackout period in connection with an individual account plan, the plan administrator shall provide timely notice of such H. R. 3763—38 blackout period to the issuer of any employer securities subject to such blackout period.

"(3) EXCEPTION FOR BLACKOUT PERIODS WITH LIMITED APPLICABILITY.—In any case in which the blackout period applies only to 1 or more participants or beneficiaries in connection with a merger, acquisition, divestiture, or similar transaction involving the plan or plan sponsor and occurs solely in connection with becoming or ceasing to be a participant or beneficiary under the plan by reason of such merger, acquisition, divestiture, or transaction, the requirement of this subsection that the notice be provided to all participants and beneficiaries shall be treated as met if the notice required under paragraph (1) is provided to such participants or beneficiaries to whom the blackout period applies as soon as reasonably practicable.

"(4) CHANGES IN LENGTH OF BLACKOUT PERIOD.—If, following the furnishing of the notice pursuant to this subsection, there is a change in the beginning date or length of the blackout period (specified in such notice pursuant to paragraph (2)(A)(iii)), the administrator shall provide affected participants and beneficiaries notice of the change as soon as reasonably practicable. In relation to the extended blackout period, such notice shall meet the requirements of paragraph (2)(D) and shall specify any material change in the matters referred to in clauses (i) through (v) of paragraph (2)(A).

"(5) REGULATORY EXCEPTIONS.—The Secretary may provide by regulation for additional exceptions to the requirements of this subsection which the Secretary determines are in the interests of participants and beneficiaries.

"(6) GUIDANCE AND MODEL NOTICES.—The Secretary shall issue guidance and model notices which meet the requirements of this subsection.

"(7) BLACKOUT PERIOD.—For purposes of this subsection—

"(A) IN GENERAL.—The term 'blackout period' means, in connection with an individual account plan, any period for which any ability of participants or beneficiaries under the plan, which is otherwise available under the terms of such plan, to direct or diversify assets credited to their accounts, to obtain loans from the plan, or to obtain distributions from the plan is temporarily suspended, limited, or restricted, if such suspension, limitation, or restriction is for any period of more than 3 consecutive business days.

"(B) EXCLUSIONS.—The term 'blackout period' does not include a suspension, limitation, or restriction—

"(i) which occurs by reason of the application of the securities laws (as defined in section 3(a)(47) of the Securities Exchange Act of 1934),

"(ii) which is a change to the plan which provides for a regularly scheduled suspension, limitation, or restriction which is disclosed to participants or beneficiaries through any summary of material modifications, any materials describing specific investment alternatives under the plan, or any changes thereto, or

"(iii) which applies only to 1 or more individuals, each of whom is the participant, an alternate payee H. R. 3763—39 (as defined in section 206(d)(3)(K)), or any other beneficiary pursuant to a qualified domestic relations order

(as defined in section 206(d)(3)(B)(i)).

"(8) INDIVIDUAL ACCOUNT PLAN —

"(A) IN GENERAL.—For purposes of this subsection, the term 'individual account plan' shall have the meaning provided such term in section 3(34), except that such term shall not include a one-participant retirement plan.

"(B) ONE-PARTICIPANT RETIREMENT PLAN.—For purposes of subparagraph (A), the term 'one-participant retirement plan' means a retirement plan that—

"(i) on the first day of the plan year—

"(I) covered only the employer (and the employer's spouse) and the employer owned the entire business (whether or not incorporated), or "(II) covered only one or more partners (and their spouses) in a business partnership (including partners in an S or C corporation (as defined in section 1361(a) of the Internal Revenue Code of 1986)), "(ii) meets the minimum coverage requirements of section 410(b) of the Internal Revenue Code of 1986 (as in effect on the date of the enactment of this paragraph) without being combined with any other plan of the business that covers the employees of the business,

"(iii) does not provide benefits to anyone except the employer (and the employer's spouse) or the partners (and their spouses),

"(iv) does not cover a business that is a member of an affiliated service group, a controlled group of corporations, or a group of businesses under common control, and

"(v) does not cover a business that leases employees."

(2) ISSUANCE OF INITIAL GUIDANCE AND MODEL NOTICE.—The Secretary of Labor shall issue initial guidance and a model notice pursuant to section 101(i)(6) of the Employee Retirement Income Security Act of 1974 (as added by this subsection) not later than January 1, 2003. Not later than 75 days after the date of the enactment of this Act, the Secretary shall promulgate interim final rules necessary to carry out the amendments made by this subsection.

(3) CIVIL PENALTIES FOR FAILURE TO PROVIDE NOTICE.—Section 502 of such Act (29 U.S.C. 1132) is amended—

(A) in subsection (a)(6), by striking "(5), or (6)" and inserting "(5), (6), or (7)";

(B) by redesignating paragraph (7) of subsection (c) as paragraph (8); and

(C) by inserting after paragraph (6) of subsection (c) the following new paragraph:

"(7) The Secretary may assess a civil penalty against a plan administrator of up to $100 a day from the date of the plan administrator's failure or refusal to provide notice to participants and beneficiaries in accordance with section 101(i). For purposes of this paragraph, each violation with respect to any single participant or beneficiary shall be treated as a separate violation.". H. R. 3763—40

(4) PLAN AMENDMENTS.—If any amendment made by this subsection requires an amendment to any plan, such plan amendment shall not be required to be made before the first plan year beginning on or after the effective date of this section, if—

(A) during the period after such amendment made by this subsection takes effect and before such first plan year, the plan is operated in good faith compliance with the requirements of such amendment made by this subsection, and

(B) such plan amendment applies retroactively to the period after such amendment made by this subsection takes effect and before such first plan year.

(c) EFFECTIVE DATE.—The provisions of this section (including the amendments made thereby) shall take effect 180 days after the date of the enactment of this Act. Good faith compliance with the requirements of such provisions in advance of the issuance of applicable regulations thereunder shall be treated as compliance with such provisions.

SEC. 307. RULES OF PROFESSIONAL RESPONSIBILITY FOR ATTORNEYS.

Not later than 180 days after the date of enactment of this Act, the Commission shall issue rules, in the public interest and for the protection of investors, setting forth minimum standards of professional conduct for attorneys appearing and practicing before the Commission in any way in the representation of issuers, including a rule—

(1) requiring an attorney to report evidence of a material violation of securities law or breach of fiduciary duty or similar violation by the company or any agent thereof, to the chief legal counsel or the chief executive officer of the company (or the equivalent thereof); and

(2) if the counsel or officer does not appropriately respond to the evidence (adopting, as necessary, appropriate remedial measures or sanctions with respect to the violation), requiring the attorney to report the evidence to the audit committee of the board of directors of the issuer or to another committee of the board of directors comprised solely of directors not employed directly or indirectly by the issuer, or to the board of directors.

SEC. 308. FAIR FUNDS FOR INVESTORS.

(a) CIVIL PENALTIES ADDED TO DISGORGEMENT FUNDS FOR THE RELIEF OF VICTIMS.

If in any judicial or administrative action brought by the Commission under the securities laws (as such term is defined in section 3(a)(47) of the Securities Exchange Act of 1934 (15 U.S.C. 78c(a)(47)) the Commission obtains an order requiring disgorgement against any person for a violation of such laws or the rules or regulations thereunder, or such person agrees in settlement of any such action to such disgorgement, and the Commission also obtains pursuant to such laws a civil penalty against such person, the amount of such civil penalty shall, on the motion or at the direction of the Commission, be added to and become part of the disgorgement fund for the benefit of the victims of such violation.

(b) ACCEPTANCE OF ADDITIONAL DONATIONS.

The Commission is authorized to accept, hold, administer, and utilize gifts, bequests and devises of property, both real and personal, to the United H. R. 3763—41

States for a disgorgement fund described in subsection (a). Such gifts, bequests, and devises of money and proceeds from sales of other property received as gifts, bequests, or devises shall be deposited in the disgorgement fund and shall be available for allocation in accordance with subsection (a).

(c) STUDY REQUIRED.—

(1) SUBJECT OF STUDY.

The Commission shall review and analyze—

(A) enforcement actions by the Commission over the five years preceding the date of the enactment of this Act that have included proceedings to obtain civil penalties or disgorgements to identify areas where such proceedings may be utilized to efficiently, effectively, and fairly provide restitution for injured investors; and (B) other methods to more efficiently, effectively, and fairly provide restitution to injured investors, including methods to improve the collection rates for civil penalties and disgorgements.

(2) REPORT REQUIRED.—The Commission shall report its findings to the Committee on Financial Services of the House of Representatives and the Committee on Banking, Housing, and Urban Affairs of the Senate within 180 days after of the date of the enactment of this Act, and shall use such findings to revise its rules and regulations as necessary. The report shall include a discussion of regulatory or legislative actions that are recommended or that may be necessary to address concerns identified in the study.

(d) CONFORMING AMENDMENTS.
Each of the following provisions is amended by inserting ", except as otherwise provided in section 308 of the Sarbanes-Oxley Act of 2002" after "Treasury of the United States":

(1) Section 21(d)(3)(C)(i) of the Securities Exchange Act of 1934 (15 U.S.C. 78u(d)(3)(C)(i)).
(2) Section 21A(d)(1) of such Act (15 U.S.C. 78u-1(d)(1)).
(3) Section 20(d)(3)(A) of the Securities Act of 1933 (15 U.S.C. 77t(d)(3)(A)).
(4) Section 42(e)(3)(A) of the Investment Company Act of 1940 (15 U.S.C. 80a–41(e)(3)(A)).
(5) Section 209(e)(3)(A) of the Investment Advisers Act of 1940 (15 U.S.C. 80b–9(e)(3)(A)).

(e) DEFINITION.
As used in this section, the term "disgorgement fund" means a fund established in any administrative or judicial proceeding described in subsection (a).

Section 301 – Public Company Audit Committees
Domain: Independence, Transparency,
Knowledge Area: Law, Ethics and Compliance, Internal and External Audit
SOX Process: Reporting and Communications, Co-ordinating Auditors

Section 301 Synopsis
The public company's Audit Committee must be independent of any other company functions and report directly to the Board of Directors.

The Public Audit Committee is responsible for:
- selecting the public auditing firm
- negotiating public auditing firm fees
- proper handling of accounting transactions

They also oversee the handling of complaints via an independent mechanism and the specifics on how to execute any reports that involve:
- internal accounting controls
- auditing methods
- treatment of accounting transactions

Criteria for the members of the audit committee:
- each Audit Committee member shall be a member of the board of directors
- besides serving on the board of directors be independent of the company
- may not accept a consulting, advisory, or other form of compensatory fee from the issuer
- may not be an affiliated person of the issuer or any subsidiary
- at least one member of the audit committee must be a financial expert

The Audit Committee also has the authority to engage independent counselors or advisers.

The Issuer should provide appropriate funding for the Audit Committee.

Section 301 GASP
APPOINTING MEMBERS TO THE AUDIT COMMITTEE

The Board of Directors should appoint at least two board members to serve on the Audit Committee. These appointees must be independent of other company functions (not actively serving in a management role within the company). In addition, the appointed members of the audit committee should have demonstrated technical expertise in finance and auditing.

It is best practice to appoint new members to the audit committee every two to three years in order to maintain independence and a fresh perspective in serving the company's financial reporting and internal control interest. When new members are admitted, it must be recorded in the notes to the committee meeting minutes and acknowledged that independence of the new member has been verified.

In the Audit Committee meeting minutes it must be recorded who is designated as the financial expert on the committee. The person delegated as the financial expert should be re-affirmed in the meeting minutes at least annually or upon any changes to positions on the committee.

REPORTING TO THE AUDIT COMMITTEE

Regularly scheduled meetings between the audit committee and internal audit, without the presence of management, should be held in order to improve communication between the two groups. This is best served by having the internal audit function report directly to the Audit Committee versus a management position within the company.

Meetings should be held at least quarterly and prior to press releases and earnings communications. These can be combined with regularly schedule meetings. Various members of management may be asked to attend in order to communicate pertinent information regarding earnings. All communications should be recorded in the meeting minutes. The meeting should also be used to address concerns raised by Internal Audit and ensure any issues are resolved in a timely manner.

RESPONSIBILITIES

The Audit Committee, Internal Audit and Chief Audit Executive should meet to discuss the requirements of this section. An implementation schedule must be developed to ensure that compliance with all parts of this section will be obtained. A tracking method must be created to confirm that actions plans approved by the Audit Committee for issues identified were, in fact, implemented as planned and monitored continuously.

The audit committee is responsible for the appointment, compensation, and oversight of the work of public accounting firm employed by the company's publicly issued financial statements. In addition, the audit committee should require that an open and competitive bidding process is completed every five years for selection of the external auditor. (See Section 203.)

The audit committee has the additional responsibility to resolve disagreements between management and the external auditor regarding GAAP, financial disclosures and technical accounting matters, in addition to the new requirement of attesting to the Internal Control environment as it relates to meeting Sarbanes-Oxley requirements. (See Section 404.)

The audit committee is responsible for establishing procedures for receiving and handling of complaints regarding accounting, internal accounting controls, or auditing matters by employees. (See Section 806 for proper handling of complaints through the Whistleblower program.) In this case, complaints of this nature must be handled and resolved by the audit committee or by the parties designated by the audit committee. The audit committee should be regularly apprised of all complaints.

At a minimum, the audit committee is responsible for reviewing and approving the following:
- company's internal audit department's charter which includes such specifics as the internal audit purpose, authority, and level or responsibility that has been approved by the audit board
- internal audit plan, especially scope and changes to internal audit activities
- internal audit's organizational structure and staffing
- internal audit budget
- on-going evaluation of risk
- a process for collecting and handling anonymous accounting and auditing related complaints
- establishment of appropriate control environment based on risk assessment

Section 302 – Corporate Responsibility for Financial Reports
Domain: Accountability
Knowledge Area: Law, Ethics and Compliance, Information Technology
SOX Process: Control Deficiencies / Remediation

Section 302 Synopsis
Section 302 focuses on managements responsibility for the design, implementation, evaluation, and reporting of disclosure controls and procedures to the SEC.

Disclosure controls and procedures are designed by a company to ensure that information required for transparency in financial reporting can be accumulated and communicated to company's management, including the CEO and CFO, in a timely manner in order to allow sufficient time for decision-making. Disclosure controls should effectively record, process, summarize and report relevant information within the time periods specified by the Commission for meeting reporting requirements.

Internal controls over financial reporting covered in Section 404 can be included within the disclosure controls covered in 302 since an issuer must maintain effective internal controls in order for the company to accurately disclose all material information in the quarterly and annual reports. Internal controls must be implemented to meet the quarterly disclosure requirements of Section 302, not only the annual financial information as required in Section 404.

The external auditor should use the same materiality considerations in an audit of internal control over financial reporting (see Section 404) as used in the audit of the companies' financial statements. Materiality in an audit of internal control over financial reporting should be applied at both the financial statement level and individual account balance level. Materiality at the individual account balance level is necessarily lower than at the financial statement level.

The certification signed by Officers of the Entity requires an assessment statement quarterly and annually, which certifies that management has evaluated and reported on the effectiveness of disclosure controls and procedures.

Management's responsibility includes:
- establishing and maintaining disclosure controls and procedures
- designing effective controls to allow awareness of all material information that needs to be reported to the SEC on a quarterly and annual basis
- evaluating the effectiveness of disclosure controls and procedures within 90 days of the issuance of the report.; in other words, management must form a current assessment, based on an evaluation within the past 90 days and not on an evaluation performed much earlier on the fiscal year
- report conclusions to the SEC based on evaluations of the effectiveness of disclosure controls and procedures

Communications with the Audit Committee and Auditors must take the following considerations into account:

- disclosure of material weaknesses
- correction of significant deficiencies
- relationship between outside auditors and the company
- required fraud reporting, whether material or immaterial, if anyone in a financial or internal control role was involved

The Certification also considers the following:
- The Officers must also certify that all disclosures have been made to both the Audit Projects and the Governance Boards that report to the CEO and CFO.
- Officers must report whether or not significant changes in internal control have taken place.
- Officers must disclose if there are any other factors that could materially affect internal controls.

Section 302 GASP
INTERNAL AUDIT CONSIDERATIONS
- Centralize the management of the internal audit function, including reporting responsibilities (see Section 301 above) as much as possible in order to create efficiencies and to ensure proper and regular communications with the audit committee.

DISCLOSURE CONTROLS

- sub-certification of key employees involved with initiating, authorizing or approving transactions affecting the financial reporting function, where the company employees certify to the CEO and CFO the same information the CEO and CFO are required to certify to the SEC
- create a disclosure committee responsible for timeliness of all reporting obligations, compliance with disclosure requirements, and internal reporting through company
- document existing company procedures before trying to assess if all significant risk are covered and if new controls need to be implemented in regard to disclosure controls
- appoint a disclosure committee to be responsible for making sure all relevant parties are informed when new controls and procedures are implemented; this committee should produce and provide training, with written reference materials to ensure compliance with all recording, timing, and disclosure requirements
- a training program should be developed to explain the requirements of the SOA and the certification process; the training should include:
    - detailed information regarding disclosure requirements
    - information regarding a tracking system for existing controls and any new controls developed
    - any control-related issues identified during testing and their remediation plans
    - a method for communicating new procedures and controls to all relevant parties as needed
    - explanation on metrics being used to track recurring findings for key controls
    - each employee's responsibility for making sure processes are accurately followed and improvements are made based on the results of testing

- arrange a regular meeting between the disclosure committee and the senior management to identify risks to anticipate issues, not just to respond to issues

CERTIFICATIONS

- Officers of the entity are required to sign a certification statement quarterly and annually reporting with the SEC that management has evaluated and reported on the effectiveness of disclosure controls and procedures. A list of these key employees should be maintained on a schedule to document receipt of certifications for each quarter.
- The company's disclosure controls and process should be documented to provide evidence of the company's compliance with the mandate to establish and evaluate quarterly disclosure controls.
- The SEC has provided forms 20-F (foreign registrants) and 40-F to be used to assist in completing the issuer's disclosure requirements. (See United States Securities and Exchange Commission: Form 20-F and Form 40-F on SEC website)
- The CEO/CFO should ensure that all steps required for certification are documented. The records should include notes describing the time and date of meeting, general descriptions of topics discussed, and a list of individuals who helped prepare and review the report. These notes should be maintained in the company's records along with the report to which the notes relate.
- As required by the certification statement signed by Officers of the issuing company, a program office should be established for the oversight of continuous improvement activities to mitigate all risks.
- The CEO and CFO are required to disclose all significant deficiencies in the design or operation of internal controls *and* any fraud involving management or employees who have a significant role in the company's internal control environment, to the company's external auditors and the audit committee of the board.

ADDITIONAL REQUIREMENTS

- All significant changes in internal control must be reported in a statement, along with any other factors that could materially affect internal controls, including remediation of significant deficiencies and material weaknesses. Any changes in internal controls should be reported to the audit committee in a timely manner. As internal audit performs testing of remediated controls previously deemed as significant deficiencies, these items can be cleared from the significant deficiency listing, as long as the control is designed and operating effectively in the current audit period.

- The company may want to establish a department to handle complaints received by the issuer regarding accounting, internal controls and other auditing matters. (See Section 301 above and Section 806.)
- Corporate counsel should keep management informed as to what constitutes a violation and the penalties to which they may be subject. (See Section 906.)
- The certification process does not require quarterly external auditors testing and relies on internal auditors testing of internal controls.
- Management may establish and sponsor a program office for oversight of continuous improvement activities to help mitigate all risks.

Section 303 – Improper Influence on Conduct of Audits

Domain: Deterrence
Knowledge Area: Ethics and Compliance, Internal and External Audit
SOX Process: Audit Compliance and Enforcement

Section 303 Synopsis

This section prohibits officers, directors, and other employees or those acting on behalf of a corporation from influencing any act that may cause a financial misstatement or may cause the financials to be materially misleading. The term extraordinary payment is defined by the court during the course of an investigation. However, in general terms, it is any payment that would not be considered ordinary, typical, normal, planned, or expected during the course of normal business.

Section 303 GASP

- The audit committee must establish, in the form of a contract with the external auditor, management's responsibility for prohibiting known acts of improper influence, of mistreating any external auditor engaged in the audit of the financial statements, for the purpose of rendering such financial statements materially misleading. The external auditor should be made aware of management's responsibilities and their method for reporting any possible violations to the audit committee.
- The audit committee should create a corporate policy that supports the reporting of these prohibited acts, addressing how questionable acts reported will be handled by the Audit Committee. (See Section 301 above.)

- In order to ensure improper influence does not occur, management should encourage their teams to provide timely and accurate information when requested by their external auditors.
- In the event of a reported violation involving an employee who has attempted to overly influence acts that are questionable as to possible misstatement of financial reports, Legal Counsel is immediately consulted and takes action to ensure facts are completely reviewed, and full co-operation by the company and the employee is maintained throughout the review of the allegation.

Section 304 – Forfeiture of Certain Bonuses and Profits

Domain: Deterrence
Knowledge Area: Accounting and Finance, Law, Ethics and Compliance
SOX Process: Audit Compliance and Enforcement

Section 304 Synopsis

If a restatement has to be filed for reasons of 'material non-compliance' the CEO and CFO must reimburse the Corporation out of their own funds for a period of twelve months from the date of issuance or filing of non-compliance documentation. Compensation to be reimbursed includes:
- **bonuses** paid by the company
- **special compensation** paid by the company
- **proceeds** from the sale of securities

Section 304 GASP

- An issuer must establish a Compensation Committee to oversee Finance, Legal and Ethic Compliance. The committee's purpose and goals for the fiscal year must be included in the annual plan.
- A communication plan must be created so that all of the officers and employees within the company know they have to comply with the repayment of funds. A training session must be provided to all officers and employees to explain the requirements. This must include a policy that requires a signed acknowledgement of their understanding of the policy by new employees upon employment with the company as a way to incorporate this into practice. A copy of this acknowledgement must be retained in the audit department, along with a copy forwarded to human resources to be kept in the employee's personnel folder.

- The audit committee is made aware of any material restatements by external auditors and takes responsibility by working closely with the compensation committee and management to enforce the policy.

Section 305 – Officer and Director Bars and Penalties
Domain: Deterrence
Knowledge Area: Law, Ethics and Compliance
SOX Process: Audit Compliance and Enforcement

Section 305 Synopsis
The Securities Exchange Act of 1934 was amended to allow Federal Courts to grant equitable relief, meaning the courts have the power to require parties to perform certain acts or specifically perform a contract, appropriate for the benefit of investors.
The SEC is allowed to prohibit someone from serving as an officer or director if that person demonstrates unfit conduct.

Section 305 GASP
- Legal counsel should review and disclose to management potential liabilities for the company on a quarterly or annual basis.
- Extensive background checks should be performed prior to an appointment to or hiring of an employee at the officer or director level.

Section 306 – Insider Trades during Pension Fund Blackout Periods
Domain: Transparency
Knowledge Area: Law, Ethics and Compliance
SOX Process: Regulations for Others, Audit Compliance

Section 306 Synopsis
Insider Trading Requirements
Section 306(a) prohibits any company director or executive from, directly or indirectly, purchasing, selling or otherwise acquiring or transferring any equity security issued by that company during a pension plan blackout period. A blackout period prevents at least 50% of the plan participants or beneficiaries from engaging in equity securities transactions through their plan accounts for a period of more than three days, if the director or officer acquired the equity security in connection with his or her service or

employment as a director or executive officer. Examples of equity securities are common shares, preferred shares and convertible securities.

ERISA Requirements

Section 306(b) requires plan administrators to furnish notices to plan participants under the Employee Retirement Income Security Act of 1974 (ERISA) who are affected by the black out period. Notices include the following information:
- reasons for the blackout period
- identification of the investments
- expected beginning date and length of the blackout period
- in the case of investments affected, a statement that the participant or beneficiary should evaluate the appropriateness of their current investment decisions in light of their inability to direct or diversify assets credited to their accounts during the blackout period
- other matters as required by regulation

Other Considerations

In addition, the rules specify the content and timing of the notice that issuers must provide to their directors and executive officers and to the Commission about a blackout period. The rules are designed to facilitate compliance with the will of Congress as reflected in Section 306(a), and to eliminate the inequities that may result when pension plan participants and beneficiaries are temporarily prevented from engaging in equity securities transactions through their plan accounts.

Exceptions

Plan administrators are required to provide 30 days advance written notice of blackout period to all plan participants or beneficiaries, with a few exceptions:
- deferral of blackout period would violate SOX (Sarbanes-Oxley) Section 404 (a) (1)
- unforeseeable emergency

Section 306 GASP
- Directors and Executives must comply with blackout policy and refrain from pension/securities transactions during this period.

- Corporate counsel must keep up with communications regarding additional guidance or exceptions.
- Plan Administrators develop plans for tracking blackout periods and issuing appropriate communication in a timely manner.
- Corporate counsel should develop a plan to monitor the Plan Administrators, to ensure compliance with blackout periods. Transactions should be tested to ensure Directors and Executives are complying with the blackout period.

Section 307 – Rules of Professional Responsibility for Attorneys
Domain: Responsibility Governance
Knowledge Area: Law, Ethics and Compliance
SOX Process: Regulations for Others

Section 307 Synopsis
Attorneys, who practice for a publicly traded company, and their subordinates are subjected to a code of ethics and responsibility.

Attorneys have the responsibility to report reporting deficiencies (see Sections 302 and 404) to the CEO and Chief Legal Counsel immediately, which should evoke corrective actions. If no actions are taken the attorney must inform the Audit Committee of the Board of Directors.

The relationship of the attorney is to represent and protect the interest of the corporation itself, and secondly to the officers or employees. Any attorney, who must appear before the commission on behalf of an issuer, first must abide by the 'Code of Ethics' when representing their client's interest, and should immediately report to the Chief Legal Counsel any acts by any member of the company that could cause a material misstatement in the financial statements. If immediate action is not taken, they are bound to take it to the Audit Committee, and ultimately if no action is taken, the attorney should report the matter to the Securities Exchange Commission.

Section 307 GASP
- Chief Legal Counsel must maintain a written 'Code of Ethics' and ensure that all attorneys assigned to work with the company acknowledge in writing their understanding of and their agreement to abide by the Code of Ethics.

- Included in the communications plan between Legal Counsel and the Audit Committee, is a signed document stating their understanding of their obligations with respect to security laws and matters supporting the proper handling and communications of violations.
- Communication with Legal Counsel should be documented in the Audit Committee meeting minutes.

Section 308 – Fair Funds for Investors
Domain: Deterrence
Knowledge Area: Law, Ethics and Compliance
SOX Process: Audit Compliance and Enforcement

Section 308 Synopsis
When violations of the federal securities acts occur involving fraud, funds invested by stockholders of the company that are to be repaid are put into disgorgement funds. Civil penalties are also added to the disgorgement funds, which are funds used to hold money that was repaid or taken back from a defendant as a result of being found guilty of violating the laws set forth in the Securities Act of 1934, and to be used for the relief of injured investors. The Securities and Exchange Commission manages the disgorgement funds. Disgorgement orders require defendants to give up the amount by which they were unjustly enriched.

The Securities and Exchange Commission seeks from the defendant, as required by the courts, an accounting of funds and other assets received by the defendant in the course of their wrongdoing in order to help the court establish the amount of money to be disgorged.

This section further requires the SEC to study and issue a report 180 days from the enactment of the SOX Act of 2002 to the Committee on Financial Services to the House of Representatives and the Committee on Banking, Housing and Urban Affairs of the Senate. The final report calls for a recommendation if further regulatory or legislative actions are needed to more fairly compensate injured investors and to identify methods to improve the collection rates for penalties and disgorgements.

Section 308 GASP
- When the Securities and Exchange Commission receives notice of misconduct, enforcement actions such as asset freezes or temporary restraining orders are obtained to help limit investor losses and increase the chance of returning funds to investors in most cases.

CHAPTER 4:
Enhanced Financial Disclosures

Practitioners Perspective and Regulation Synopsis

Title IV covers all aspects of Financial Disclosure for the SOX Act. From a practitioner's perspective, Sections 401, 404, and 409 are the key areas prescribing much of the practitioner's focus and activity towards implementation of the Act. Section 401 requires specific financial statement disclosures related to material correcting adjustments, off-balance sheet transactions, pro-forma figures, and special purpose entities. Section 404 requires management assessment and reporting on internal control over financial reporting, as well as a requirement that public accounting firms attest to management's assessment of internal control effectiveness. Section 409 mandates that material changes are disclosed to the public on a real-time basis.

Regulation Text

SEC. 401. DISCLOSURES IN PERIODIC REPORTS.
(a) DISCLOSURES REQUIRED. - Section 13 of the Securities Exchange Act of 1934 (15 U.S.C. 78m) is amended by adding at the end the following:
   "(i) ACCURACY OF FINANCIAL REPORTS. - Each financial report that contains financial statements, and that is required to be prepared in accordance with (or reconciled to) generally accepted accounting principles under this title and filed with the Commission shall reflect all material correcting adjustments that have been identified by a registered public accounting firm in accordance with generally accepted accounting principles and the rules and regulations of the Commission.

"(j) OFF-BALANCE SHEET TRANSACTIONS. - Not later than 180 days after the date of enactment of the Sarbanes-Oxley Act of 2002, the Commission shall issue final rules providing that each annual and quarterly financial report required to be filed with the Commission shall disclose all material off-balance sheet transactions, arrangements, obligations (including contingent obligations), and other relationships of the issuer with unconsolidated entities or other persons, that may have a material current or future effect on financial condition, changes in financial condition, results of operations, liquidity, capital expenditures, capital resources, or significant components of revenues or expenses."

(b) COMMISSION RULES ON PRO-FORMA FIGURES. - Not later than 180 days after the date of enactment of the Sarbanes-Oxley Act of 2002, the Commission shall issue final rules providing that pro-forma financial information included in any periodic or other report filed with the Commission pursuant to the securities laws, or in any public disclosure or press or other release, shall be presented in a manner that -

(1) does not contain an untrue statement of a material fact or omit to state a material fact necessary in order to make the pro-forma financial information, in light of the circumstances under which it is presented, not misleading; and

(2) reconciles it with the financial condition and results of operations of the issuer under generally accepted accounting principles.

(c) STUDY AND REPORT ON SPECIAL PURPOSE ENTITIES. -

(1) STUDY REQUIRED. - The Commission shall, not later than 1 year after the effective date of adoption of off-balance sheet disclosure rules required by section 13(j) of the Securities Exchange Act of 1934, as added by this section, complete a study of filings by issuers and their disclosures to determine -

(A) the extent of off-balance sheet transactions, including assets, liabilities, leases, losses, and the use of special purpose entities; and

(B) whether generally accepted accounting rules result in financial statements of issuers reflecting the economics of such off-balance sheet transactions to investors in a transparent fashion.

(2) REPORT AND RECOMMENDATIONS. - Not later than 6 months after the date of completion of the study required by paragraph (1), the Commission shall submit a report to the President, the Committee on Banking, Housing, and Urban Affairs of the Senate, and the Committee on Financial Services of the House of Representatives, setting forth -

(A) the amount or an estimate of the amount of off-balance sheet transactions, including assets, liabilities, leases, and losses of, and the use of special purpose entities by, issuers filing periodic reports pursuant to section 13 or 15 of the Securities Exchange Act of 1934;

(B) the extent to which special purpose entities are used to facilitate off-balance sheet transactions;

(C) whether generally accepted accounting principles or the rules of the Commission result in financial statements of issuers reflecting the economics of such transactions to investors in a transparent fashion;

(D) whether generally accepted accounting principles specifically result in the consolidation of special purpose entities sponsored by an issuer in cases in which the issuer has the majority of the risks and rewards of the special purpose entity; and

(E) any recommendations of the Commission for improving the transparency and quality of reporting off-balance sheet transactions in the financial statements and disclosures required to be filed by an issuer with the Commission.

SEC. 402. ENHANCED CONFLICT OF INTEREST PROVISIONS.

(a) PROHIBITION ON PERSONAL LOANS TO EXECUTIVES. - Section 13 of the Securities Exchange Act of 1934 (15 U.S.C. 78m), as amended by this Act, is amended by adding at the end the following:

"(k) PROHIBITION ON PERSONAL LOANS TO EXECUTIVES. -

"(1) IN GENERAL. - It shall be unlawful for any issuer (as defined in section 2 of the Sarbanes-Oxley Act of 2002), directly or indirectly, including through any subsidiary, to extend or maintain credit, to arrange for the extension of credit, or to renew an extension of credit, in the form of a personal loan to or for any director or executive officer (or equivalent thereof) of that issuer. An extension of credit maintained by the issuer on the date of enactment of this subsection shall not be subject to the provisions of this subsection, provided that there is no material modification to any term of any such extension of credit or any renewal of any such extension of credit on or after that date of enactment.

"(2) LIMITATION. - Paragraph (1) does not preclude any home improvement and manufactured home loans (as that term is defined in section 5 of the Home Owners' Loan Act (12 U.S.C. 1464)), consumer credit (as defined in section 103 of the Truth in Lending Act (15 U.S.C. 1602)), or any extension of credit under an open end credit plan (as defined in section 103 of the Truth in Lending Act (15 U.S.C. 1602)), or a charge card (as defined in section 127(c)(4)(e) of the Truth in Lending Act (15 U.S.C. 1637(c)(4)(e)), or any extension of credit by a broker or dealer registered under section 15 of this title to an employee of that broker or dealer to buy, trade, or carry securities, that is permitted under rules or regulations of the Board of Governors of the Federal Reserve System pursuant to section 7 of this title (other than an extension of credit that would be used to purchase the stock of that issuer), that is -

"(A) made or provided in the ordinary course of the consumer credit business of such issuer;

"(B) of a type that is generally made available by such issuer to the public; and

"(C) made by such issuer on market terms, or terms that are no more favorable than those offered by the issuer to the general public for such extensions of credit.

"(3) RULE OF CONSTRUCTION FOR CERTAIN LOANS. - Paragraph (1) does not apply to any loan made or maintained by an insured depository institution (as defined in section 3 of the Federal Deposit Insurance Act (12 U.S.C. 1813)), if the loan is subject to the insider lending restrictions of section 22(h) of the Federal Reserve Act (12 U.S.C. 375b).".

SEC. 403. DISCLOSURES OF TRANSACTIONS INVOLVING MANAGEMENT AND PRINCIPAL STOCKHOLDERS.

(a) AMENDMENT. - Section 16 of the Securities Exchange Act of 1934 (15 U.S.C. 78p) is amended by striking the heading of such section and subsection (a) and inserting the following:

"SEC. 16. DIRECTORS, OFFICERS, AND PRINCIPAL STOCKHOLDERS.

"(a) DISCLOSURES REQUIRED. -

"(1) DIRECTORS, OFFICERS, AND PRINCIPAL STOCKHOLDERS REQUIRED TO FILE. - Every person who is directly or indirectly the beneficial owner of more than 10 percent of any class of any equity security (other than an exempted security) which is registered pursuant to section 12, or who is a director or an officer of the issuer of such security, shall file the statements required by this subsection with the Commission (and, if such security is registered on a national securities exchange, also with the exchange).

"(2) TIME OF FILING. - The statements required by this subsection shall be filed -

"(A) at the time of the registration of such security on a national securities exchange or by the effective date of a registration statement filed pursuant to section 12(g);

"(B) within 10 days after he or she becomes such beneficial owner, director, or officer;

"(C) if there has been a change in such ownership, or if such person shall have purchased or sold a security-based swap agreement (as defined in section 206(b) of the Gramm-Leach-Bliley Act (15 U.S.C. 78c note)) involving such equity security, before the end of the second business day following the day on which the subject transaction has been executed, or at such other time as the Commission shall establish, by rule, in any case in which the Commission determines that such 2-day period is not feasible.

"(3) CONTENTS OF STATEMENTS. - A statement filed -

"(A) under subparagraph (A) or (B) of paragraph (2) shall contain a statement of the amount of all equity securities of such issuer of which the filing person is the beneficial owner; and

"(B) under subparagraph (C) of such paragraph shall indicate ownership by the filing person at the date of filing, any such changes in such ownership, and such purchases and sales of the security-based swap agreements as have occurred since the most recent such filing under such subparagraph.

"(4) ELECTRONIC FILING AND AVAILABILITY. - Beginning not later than 1 year after the date of enactment of the Sarbanes-Oxley Act of 2002 -

"(A) a statement filed under subparagraph (C) of paragraph (2) shall be filed electronically;

"(B) the Commission shall provide each such statement on a publicly accessible Internet site not later than the end of the business day following that filing; and

"(C) the issuer (if the issuer maintains a corporate website) shall provide that statement on that corporate website, not later than the end of the business day following that filing."

(b) EFFECTIVE DATE. - The amendment made by this section shall be effective 30 days after the date of the enactment of this Act.

SEC. 404. MANAGEMENT ASSESSMENT OF INTERNAL CONTROLS.

(a) RULES REQUIRED. - The Commission shall prescribe rules requiring each annual report required by section 13(a) or 15(d) of the Securities Exchange Act of 1934 (15 U.S.C. 78m or 78o(d)) to contain an internal control report, which shall -
(1) state the responsibility of management for establishing and maintaining an adequate internal control structure and procedures for financial reporting; and
(2) contain an assessment, as of the end of the most recent fiscal year of the issuer, of the effectiveness of the internal control structure and procedures of the issuer for financial reporting.

(b) INTERNAL CONTROL EVALUATION AND REPORTING. - With respect to the internal control assessment required by subsection (a), each registered public accounting firm that prepares or issues the audit report for the issuer shall attest to, and report on, the assessment made by the management of the issuer. An attestation made under this subsection shall be made in accordance with standards for attestation engagements issued or adopted by the Board. Any such attestation shall not be the subject of a separate engagement.

SEC. 405. EXEMPTION.

Nothing in section 401, 402, or 404, the amendments made by those sections, or the rules of the Commission under those sections shall apply to any investment company registered under section 8 of the Investment Company Act of 1940 (15 U.S.C. 80a-8).

SEC. 406. CODE OF ETHICS FOR SENIOR FINANCIAL OFFICERS.

(a) CODE OF ETHICS DISCLOSURE. - The Commission shall issue rules to require each issuer, together with periodic reports required pursuant to section 13(a) or 15(d) of the Securities Exchange Act of 1934, to disclose whether or not, and if not, the reason therefore, such issuer has adopted a code of ethics for senior financial officers, applicable to its principal financial officer and comptroller or principal accounting officer, or persons performing similar functions.

(b) CHANGES IN CODES OF ETHICS. - The Commission shall revise its regulations concerning matters requiring prompt disclosure on Form 8-K (or any successor thereto) to require the immediate disclosure, by means of the filing of such form, dissemination by the Internet or by other electronic means, by any issuer of any change in or waiver of the code of ethics for senior financial officers.

(c) DEFINITION. - In this section, the term "code of ethics" means such standards as are reasonably necessary to promote -
    (1) honest and ethical conduct, including the ethical handling of actual or apparent conflicts of interest between personal and professional relationships;
    (2) full, fair, accurate, timely, and understandable disclosure in the periodic reports required to be filed by the issuer; and
    (3) compliance with applicable governmental rules and regulations.

(d) DEADLINE FOR RULEMAKING. - The Commission shall -
    (1) propose rules to implement this section, not later than 90 days after the date of enactment of this Act; and
    (2) issue final rules to implement this section, not later than 180 days after that date of enactment.

SEC. 407. DISCLOSURE OF AUDIT COMMITTEE FINANCIAL EXPERT.

(a) RULES DEFINING "FINANCIAL EXPERT". - The Commission shall issue rules, as necessary or appropriate in the public interest and consistent with the protection of investors, to require each issuer, together with periodic reports required pursuant to sections 13(a) and 15(d) of the Securities Exchange Act of 1934, to disclose whether or not, and if not, the reasons therefore, the audit committee of that issuer is comprised of at least 1 member who is a financial expert, as such term is defined by the Commission.

(b) CONSIDERATIONS. - In defining the term "financial expert" for purposes of subsection (a), the Commission shall consider whether a person has, through education and experience as a public accountant or auditor or a principal financial officer, comptroller, or principal accounting officer of an issuer, or from a position involving the performance of similar functions -
   (1) an understanding of generally accepted accounting principles and financial statements;
   (2) experience in -
      (A) the preparation or auditing of financial statements of generally comparable issuers; and
      (B) the application of such principles in connection with the accounting for estimates, accruals, and reserves;
   (3) experience with internal accounting controls; and
   (4) an understanding of audit committee functions.

(c) DEADLINE FOR RULEMAKING. - The Commission shall -
   (1) propose rules to implement this section, not later than 90 days after the date of enactment of this Act; and
   (2) issue final rules to implement this section, not later than 180 days after that date of enactment.

SEC. 408. ENHANCED REVIEW OF PERIODIC DISCLOSURES BY ISSUERS.

(a) REGULAR AND SYSTEMATIC REVIEW. - The Commission shall review disclosures made by issuers reporting under section 13(a) of the Securities Exchange Act of 1934 (including reports filed on Form 10-K), and which have a class of securities listed on a national securities exchange or traded on an automated quotation facility of a national securities association, on a regular and systematic basis for the protection of investors. Such review shall include a review of an issuer's financial statement.

(b) REVIEW CRITERIA. - For purposes of scheduling the reviews required by subsection (a), the Commission shall consider, among other factors -
   (1) issuers that have issued material restatements of financial results;
   (2) issuers that experience significant volatility in their stock price as compared to other issuers;
   (3) issuers with the largest market capitalization;
   (4) emerging companies with disparities in price to earning ratios;

(5) issuers whose operations significantly affect any material sector of the economy; and

(6) any other factors that the Commission may consider relevant.

(c) MINIMUM REVIEW PERIOD. - In no event shall an issuer required to file reports under section 13(a) or 15(d) of the Securities Exchange Act of 1934 be reviewed under this section less frequently than once every 3 years.

SEC. 409. REAL TIME ISSUER DISCLOSURES.
Section 13 of the Securities Exchange Act of 1934 (15 U.S.C. 78m), as amended by this Act, is amended by adding at the end the following:

"(l) REAL TIME ISSUER DISCLOSURES. - Each issuer reporting under section 13(a) or 15(d) shall disclose to the public on a rapid and current basis such additional information concerning material changes in the financial condition or operations of the issuer, in plain English, which may include trend and qualitative information and graphic presentations, as the Commission determines, by rule, is necessary or useful for the protection of investors and in the public interest.".

Section 401 – Disclosures in Periodic Reports

Domain: Accountability, Responsibility, transparency
Knowledge Area: Accounting and Finance
SOX Process: Reporting and Communication

Section 401 Synopsis

In order to provide for transparency in financial reporting, this section addresses accuracy in presenting financial reports with specific instructions for disclosing complex transactions and pro-forma figures. Financial statements filed with the SEC must meet the following requirements:

- conform, or be reconciled, to GAAP
- issuers who do not report under GAAP must explain why
- international operations who report under a different standard must be aware of their responsibility to reconcile their reporting method to GAAP practices
- final report must include all adjusting entries identified by the registered public accounting firm
- include off-balance sheet transactions, including assets, liabilities, leases, and losses of, and the use of special purpose entities

- pro-forma figures include disclosing assumptions built into the reported data, and expected results that are possible if the assumptions used turn out to be true

Section 401 GASP
- GAAP principles must be applied consistently throughout all financial reports.
- Other accounting standards used for financial reporting must be reconciled back to GAAP, or an explanation of the differences must be disclosed.
- Financial reporting personnel must establish processes and procedures to identify and report material correcting adjustments, off-balance sheet transactions, pro-forma figures and special purpose entities in compliance with SEC requirements.
- Prior to signing off on financial reports, the Chief Financial Officer must make sure all correcting adjustments provided by the public accounting firm have been incorporated into the final copy of the financial statement.
- The Chief Financial Officer establishes accounting policies to ensure that the following objectives are met:
    - reduce complexity in accounting transactions to reflect true economic activity
    - reduce complexity in accounting standards to be more objective
    - improve consistency of disclosures
    - improve overall communications in financial reporting
- Specific and clearly stated accounting standards must be established and publicly disclosed related to the following:
    - consolidation of entities
    - defined benefit pension plans
    - accounting for leases
    - fair value accounting
- The Chief Financial Officer takes responsibility for educating company directors and managers of the importance of recognizing any guaranteed contract that could potentially be required for disclosure as future, long-term liabilities.

- The Chief Financial Officer executes due care in presenting pro-forma financial statements to make sure that any assumptions of a material nature would not present misleading or incorrect information to the public. In addition, pro-forma financials statements are reconciled to the actual results of operations stated according to GAAP.

Section 402 – Enhanced Conflict of Interest Provisions
Domain: Transparency
Knowledge Area: Accounting and Finance, Law, Ethics and Compliance, Internal and External Audit
SOX Process: Reporting and Communication

Section 402 Synopsis
Personal loans to directors and executive officers are prohibited with the exception of:
- loans made during the ordinary course of the issuer's business
- loans offered to the public
- loans made in accordance with market terms or conditions
- loans for home improvement – as defined in Home Owners Loan Act
- consumer credit – as defined in Truth in Lending Act
- extension of credit to a registered Broker or Dealer permitted under the rules and regulations of the Board of Governors of the Federal Reserve System
- charge cards – as defined in Truth in Lending Act
- loans that meet the requirements for insider lending restrictions according to the Federal Reserve Act for FDIC institutions

Section 402 GASP
- A formal prohibition included in the code of ethics or similar policy should be established to specifically restrict personal loans with associated compliance processes and practices.
- Internal Audit and/or Legal should conduct a periodic audit of loan processes and terms.
- Any officer or director loans should be properly disclosed in the financial reporting.

Section 403 – Disclosures of Transactions Involving Management and Principal Stockholders

Domain: Accountability, Responsibility, Transparency
Knowledge Area: Accounting and Finance
SOX Process: Reporting and Communication

Section 403 Synopsis

Beneficial owners or 'insiders' must file statements with the Securities Exchange Commission whenever they buy, sell, trade or acquire stocks. A beneficial owner or insider is defined as:
- issuing company directors, or officers
- individuals who directly or indirectly own more than 10% of any class of the issuing company's stock, security or equity

The statements must list the quantity and value of stocks and who owns them.

When filing a statement with the Commission, the following deadlines apply:
- When an issuer is required to register with the SEC to comply with section 12(g) of the Securities Exchange Act of 1934, (ie because it has engaged in interstate commerce, has assets exceeding $1 million, and 500 or more persons hold that class of security), beneficial owners and insiders must file a statement with the SEC at the time of registration.
- When an individual has recently become a beneficial owner, they must file a statement within 10 days of the transaction.
- When an individual has acquired stocks via an individually negotiated swap agreement, the insider must file Form 3 (initial statement of beneficial ownership of securities), Form 4 (statement of changes in beneficial ownership of securities), and/or Form 5 (annual statement of beneficial ownership of securities).

The beneficial owner or insider must file forms 3, 4, and 5 using the SEC's Electronic Gathering, Analysis and Retrieval system (EDGAR). The issuing company must then provide the same forms on their corporate website within one business day of filing.

Section 403 GASP
- Financial reporting personnel need to establish processes and procedures to identify/monitor ownership changes, particularly for directors and officers of the company, for timely public disclosure.

- Further detail rules from the PCAOB, related to both the stock transaction triggers and timeliness of reporting should be referenced. (See PCAOB Staff Audit Practice Alert No. 1 MATTERS RELATED TO TIMING AND ACCOUNTING FOR OPTION GRANTS, July 28, 2006.)
- Audit Committee and internal auditors need to be made aware of any possibility of the company's actual practices in granting stock options including the 'backdating' of such grants that have been inconsistent with the manner in which these transactions were initially recorded and disclosed. Lacking the proper accounting and disclosure for stock option grants could lead to a material misstatement in the financial statements or lead the external auditors to conclude that there are significant deficiencies in its Internal Control over Financial Reporting (ICOFR). Therefore PCAOB Alert No. 1 provides Management and auditors with additional guidance when considering the impact of stock options on their reporting requirements:
  - application of financial accounting standards
  - consideration of materiality
  - possibility of illegal acts
- Using SEC's online Electronic Gathering, Analysis and Retrieval system (EDGAR), beneficial owners must file:
  - **Form 3** when purchasing or acquiring stock
  - **Form 4** whenever changes in stock ownership occur
  - **Form 5** annually
- Beneficial owners must notify the issuing company whenever Form(s) 3, 4, and/or 5 is filed with the SEC.
- Issuing companies must post Form(s) 3, 4, and/or 5 on their company website within 1 business day of filing.

Section 404 – Management Assessment of Internal Controls
Domain: Accountability, Transparency, Governance
Knowledge Area: Accounting and Finance, Information Technology, Internal and External Audit
SOX Process: Planning, Risk Assessment, Control Assessment, Control Testing, Control Deficiencies / Remediation, Reporting and Communication, Evaluation, Sustaining

Section 404 Synopsis

Section 404 requires that all annual financial statements report on the effectiveness of the Internal Control Over Financial Reporting (ICOFR) with a statement of management's responsibility for maintaining an 'adequate' internal control environment. Management's assessment of the effectiveness of the control structure should disclose any weaknesses in these controls within the annual reports. In addition, the company's certified external auditors will attest to the accuracy of the company management's assertion that internal accounting controls are in place, operational, and effective. This requirement is no longer mandated as a result of the release of Audit Standard 5. (See below for details.)

Public accounting firms that prepare or issue the audit report accompanying the company's annual reports must also attest to, and report on, the assessment of internal controls made by management.

(a) Rules Required. The Commission shall prescribe rules requiring each annual report required by section 13(a) or 15(d) of the Securities Exchange Act of 1934 to contain an internal control report, which shall:

(1) state management's responsibility for establishing and maintaining an adequate internal control structure and procedures for financial reporting

(2) contain an assessment, as of the end of the most recent fiscal year of the issuer, of the effectiveness of the internal control structure and procedures of the issuer for financial reporting

(b) Internal Control Evaluation and Reporting. With respect to the internal control assessment required by subsection (a), each certified public accounting firm that prepares or issues the audit report for the company shall attest to, and report on, the assessment made by the management of the issuer. An attestation made under this subsection shall be made in accordance with standards for attestation engagements issued or adopted by the PCAOB Board.

NEW AUDIT STANDARD

On May 24, 2007, the PCAOB adopted Auditing Standard No. 5, An Audit of Internal Control Over Financial Reporting that is integrated with An Audit of Financial Statements. The new standard will apply to audits of all companies required by SEC rules to obtain an audit of internal controls.

The new standard results from the Board's monitoring of auditors' implementation of Auditing Standard No. 2, through, among other things, inspections of internal control audits and public roundtable discussions held in April 2005 and May 2006. While the Board observed significant benefits produced by the audit, including higher quality financial reporting, it also noted that, at times, the related effort has appeared greater than necessary to conduct an effective audit. Based on these observations, and in light of the approaching date for smaller companies to comply with the Act's internal control reporting requirements, the Board proposed (for public comment) a new standard on auditing internal controls.

Audit Standard No. 5 was designed to achieve four objectives:

- **Focus the Internal Control Audit on the most important matters** – The new standard focuses auditors on those areas that present the greatest risk that a company's internal control will fail to prevent or detect a material misstatement in the financial statements. The standard does so by incorporating certain best practices designed to focus the scope of the audit on identifying material weaknesses in internal control, before they result in material misstatements of financial statements, such as using a top-down approach to planning the audit. The standard also emphasizes the importance of auditing higher risk areas, such as the financial statement close process and controls designed to prevent fraud by management. At the same time, the standard provides auditors with a range of alternatives for addressing lower risk areas, such as by more clearly demonstrating how to calibrate the nature, timing, and extent of testing based on risk. The standard encourages auditors to incorporate knowledge accumulated in previous years' audits into the auditors' assessment of risk and use the work performed by companies' own personnel, when appropriate.

- **Eliminate procedures that are unnecessary to achieve the intended benefits** – The Board examined every area of the internal control audit to determine whether the previous standard encouraged auditors to perform procedures that are not necessary to achieve the intended benefits of the audit. The new standard does not include Audit Standard No. 2's detailed requirements to evaluate management's own evaluation process, and clarifies that an internal control audit does not require an opinion on the adequacy of management's process. The new standard refocuses the multi-location direction on risk rather than coverage by removing the requirement that auditors test a 'large portion' of the company's operations or financial position.
- **Make the Audit clearly scalable to fit the size and the complexity of any company** – In co-ordination with the Board's ongoing project, the new standard explains how to tailor internal control audits to fit the size and complexity of the company being audited. The new standard developed guidance for auditors of smaller, less complex companies, by including notes throughout the standard on how to apply the principles in the standard to smaller, less complex companies. The standard also includes a discussion of the relevant attributes of smaller, less complex companies as well as less complex units of larger companies.
- **Simplify the text of the standard** – The Board's new standard is shorter and easier to read because it uses simpler terms to describe procedures and definitions. In order to better co-ordinate the final standard and the SEC's new rules and management guidance, the new standard conforms certain terms to the SEC's rules and guidance, such as the definition of 'material weakness' and use of the term 'entity-level controls' instead of 'company-level controls.'

The new standard:
- aligns key terms and concepts with terms used in SEC rules and guidance
- includes a discussion of fraud risk and anti-fraud controls at the beginning of the standard, to emphasize the importance of these matters in assessing risk
- explains how different kinds of entity-level controls have different effects on the selection and testing of controls; for example, entity-level controls that monitor the operation of other controls in a precise manner may reduce the need for testing of the underlying, process-level controls

- focuses auditors on fulfilling the objectives that a properly performed walkthrough achieves, rather than requiring performance of a walkthrough, which, under some circumstances, might lead to a checklist approach
- emphasizes that auditors need not scope the audit to find deficiencies that, individually or when aggregated with other deficiencies, do not constitute material weaknesses; at the same time, the standard retains the requirements to evaluate all deficiencies that are identified and communicate both material weaknesses and significant deficiencies, in writing, to the audit committee
- instead of adopting the proposed standard on considering and using the work of others, the Board retained AU sec. 322, The Auditor's Consideration of the Internal Audit Function in an Audit of Financial Statements; in light of this decision, consistent with the Board's intent in the proposal, the new standard itself expressly permits auditors to use, in the internal control audit, testing and other internal control work of persons other than internal auditors
- the standard allows auditors to tailor their top-down approach to the circumstances of individual companies by removing the requirement to specifically identify major classes of transactions and significant processes before identifying relevant assertions

Section 404 GASP

These GASP Statements are best practices to help companies align their '404 Implementation' with their auditor's expectations as detailed by the PCAOB Audit Standards 1 -5. These statements are organized into the following sub-sections:

1. Introduction
2. Development of Project Plan
3. Mapping of Significant Accounts
4. Sub Processes and Financial Statement Assertions
5. Identification of Technology Supporting Key Business Processes
6. Determining Materiality
7. Entity Level Controls
8. Documentation of Business Process and Controls
9. Process Walkthroughs
10. Test of Operating Effectiveness

11. Results – Reporting Deficiencies
12. Remediation
13. Management Reporting
14. Evaluating IT General Controls.
15. Outside Processors

INTRODUCTION
Meeting the requirements of Section 404 requires a rigorous process, with carefully managed resources and expertise. The PCAOB has called for a top-down, risk based, integrated audit approach in internal controls over financial reporting.

DEVELOPMENT OF PROJECT PLAN
- Companies face a rigid deadline once they are required to meet the reporting requirements of Section 404. Begin by planning and scoping accordingly, taking the time to understand which business processes and IT applications are relevant to financial reporting. Your plan should only include those processes and applications which were deemed material and relevant.
- A top down approach to planning the audit helps to ensure material weaknesses in internal control are identified before they lead to misstatements in reporting of financial statements. This approach fits within Audit Standard No. 5 issued in May of 2007.
- Identify dedicated resources and determine the amount of time that will be devoted exclusively to the SOX project. Resources should include a project manager, internal audit staff, the CFO, and process owners from each identified business process area. Also include the external auditors to be sure they approve of your approach.
- The project plan should include identification of significant accounts, review of current documentation, performance of a risk assessment, a gap analysis, creation of any new documentation required after analysis, tests of controls, remediation, and creation of a plan to monitor the processes going forward once the initial project is complete.
- A project manager (PM) for a 404 readiness program will have a background in financial reporting, financial controls and financial systems. With the defined deadline for SOX 404 reporting, the PM must be able to manage schedules and tasks while dealing with all of the critical decisions that occur throughout the course of the project. An experienced

project manager familiar with PM principles, a PM certification and prior financial experience is needed. An internal person should hold the role of PM as that person will have a good understanding of how the business is run and have a stake in the outcome. For a small company, if an internal candidate is not qualified, then a consultant resource with verifiable previous SOX 404 implementation experience in your industry or a closely related industry is strongly encouraged.
- For smaller companies it is usually necessary to engage outside consulting resources to complete some or most of the tasks, but it is best if the overall project management is controlled by an internal resource to ensure the company's best interests are considered.
- According to the PCAOB, performing an overall risk assessment during the initial planning phase allows for improved decision-making when addressing lower risk areas, such as how to incorporate lessons learned from previous years' audits into the auditors' assessment of risk, and when and where to use the work performed by the company's own personnel.

MAPPING OF SIGNIFICANT ACCOUNTS
- Significant Accounts are those that can affect the financial statements in a material way. Look at the balance sheet, income statement, statement of cash flows, notes and other disclosures to find those accounts. Complete a risk assessment to determine what accounts have several controls and where a breakdown could realistically create a materiality issue.

SUB-PROCESS AND FINANCIAL STATEMENT ASSERTIONS
- Sub Processes that support significant accounts and financial statement assertions will help determine what is in scope. It helps to have a checklist or chart of some kind to map sub processes to significant accounts and what financial assertions are applicable. A visual of complete information tells you that the process is in scope. An incomplete visual tells you that a particular process is probably not in scope and you should consider dropping it from the review.
- Each significant account should have one or more financial statement assertions assigned. These assertions serve as the basis for management's assessment of the financial reporting process. A list of Financial Statement Assertions are as follows:
  - existence/occurrence
  - completeness

- valuation
- rights and obligations
- presentation and disclosure

IDENTIFICATION OF TECHNOLOGY AND APPLICATIONS SUPPORTING KEY PROCESSES

- Make an inventory all of the software applications and determine which business processes are supported by each application. Any application that provides support to significant accounts such as complicated calculations, on-line revenue streams, inventory balances, and fixed assets are definitely in scope. Incorporating supporting applications into a checklist or visual will help in deciding what is in scope.
- Based on the in-scope applications, identify the higher level technology that supports each application. This information will later be used in the review of IT General Controls, and needs to identify the applications software (ERP and other Applications), source of the application (In-house or purchased), operating system it sits on, network operating system that initially authenticates users to the system and underlying database which houses the data used in the application.
- If any of the above applications are outsourced through a third party service provider, these should also be documented along with the location of the provider.

DETERMINING MATERIALITY

- The PCAOB has defined criteria for identifying significant accounts in Audit Standard No. 2:
    - The auditor should identify significant accounts and disclosures, first at the financial-statement level, and then at the account or disclosure-component level. Determining specific controls to test begins by identifying significant accounts and disclosures within the financial statements. When identifying significant accounts, the auditor should evaluate both quantitative and qualitative factors.
    - An account is significant if there is more than a remote likelihood that the account could contain misstatements that individually, or when aggregated with others, could have a material effect on the financial statements, considering the risks of both overstatement and understatement. Other accounts may be significant on a qualitative basis based on the expectations of a reasonable user.

- Based on the PCAOB criteria, management should establish realistic guidelines in evaluating the materiality of accounts affecting the financial statements:
  - Determine the material accounts that have the greatest risk of causing a significant misstatement in the issuance of the financial statements.
  - Then define the criteria used, either as a percentage or an absolute dollar value that meet a reasonable standard.
  - Set the level to the smallest amount that would cause a significant misrepresentation in the company's financial statements. This assessment is based on the likelihood of something going wrong and what level of risk the auditor is willing to accept.
  - Document the rational and be sure the external auditors agree with the approach.
- Take the balance sheet and income statement to perform an analysis of significant accounts. The analysis consists of determining the materiality of each significant account in relation to the total. Balance sheet accounts materiality would be based on a percentage of total assets and total equity. Income statement accounts materiality would be based on a percentage of total revenues. When determining significant accounts one must document each conclusion. Any accounts that are immaterial should be documented as such and would not require further evaluation and testing of key controls. (See Appendix A – Mapping of Significant Accounts.)
- Pay particular attention to any accounts that are determined by estimations, ie Deferred Income Taxes, as they could easily be misreported. In this case, all balances derived with high degree of estimating should be included no matter what the significance of the balance.
- Once significant accounts are determined, involve external auditors in the review of the conclusions and assumptions made, to ensure that there is an agreement as to the approach.

ENTITY LEVEL CONTROLS
- Regardless of the size of the organization there are entity level controls that will apply. Referred to as 'Tone at The Top', these controls permeate throughout an organization. For example, the 'Tone at The Top' may include:
  - policy and procedure statements
  - a code of ethics (which is required by SOX)

    - a code of conduct
    - required passwords to access an application
    - less tangible concepts like culture and the tone demonstrated by management
- The most widely accepted internal control framework is the one issued by The Committee of Sponsoring Organizations of the Treadway Commission (COSO), which when fully implemented will provide a well controlled environment.
- Management may use a framework other than COSO, if the framework selected is a suitable, recognized control framework. Even if a company does not follow all of the concepts of COSO, there is still some benefit in understanding the concepts behind COSO and what controls can be applied to the organization.
- All Entity Level Controls should be reviewed and documented as they will serve as a significant part of the assessment of Internal Control of Financial Reporting. (See Appendix B – Entity Level Controls.) A representative list of examples include:
    - Board of Directors and Audit Committee
    - Integrity and Ethical Values statements
    - Human Resources Policies
    - Organizational Structure
    - Management's Operating Style
    - Commitment to Competence
    - Assignment of Responsibility
    - Strategic Planning
    - Organizational Risk Assessment
    - Corporate Policies and Procedures
    - Information Technology Systems
    - Budgeting and Analysis
    - Internal Audit Activities

DOCUMENTATION OF BUSINESS PROCESSES AND CONTROLS

- The documentation of business processes and controls can be one of the more intensive parts of the project requiring dedicated resources and expertise. The documentation is usually organized by logical business process groupings around the core business, such as Order to Cash, Procure to Pay, Plan to Produce, Payroll, etc. In addition, Corporate Administrative Services covering long-term liabilities in the areas of Pensions, Taxes, and Retiree Benefits should be documented separately.
- Section 404 requires sufficient documentation of the business processes including control points and flow of transactions through the system. This should be developed in such a way that a reader without prior knowledge of the business could easily understand the general flow of how the process operates. The different forms of documentation produced at this stage includes:
    - **Flowcharts** – graphical depiction of the process flow, divided into swim lanes by each responsible department or individual (See Appendix C – Flowcharts.)
    - **Narratives** – textual description of the business process from start through end

It is up to each company to determine the appropriate level of detail required so long as it satisfies the requirements stated above. The two forms of documentation above can be combined into one document, if desired, to make it easier for on-going maintenance. It is also important that the documentation remain consistent across all business units and process areas. IT would also need to follow this practice with some noted exceptions. (See ITGC below.)

- Standard templates for completing the documentation should be prepared by the Project Manager and sent to the project team at the start of this phase. Control over the documents as they are completed is also an essential part of the project manager's duties. In addition, the project manager needs to schedule interviews with the process owners and ensure that there is sufficient time to complete the documentation of their areas of responsibility.
- Each step in the process needs to be documented to include: who performs (by position Title), steps to complete, who reviews, who signs off, etc. Each step or activity in the process should be numbered and cross-referenced to other documentation produced, including a risk and control matrix (R&CM) and a flowchart.

- Segregation of Duties (SOD) is an important control objective that is evaluated throughout each process. Based on the review of the business process, documenting any potential SOD violations can be very useful if completed early on, and becomes useful during other phases of the project, such as testing, remediation and evaluation control deficiencies. This document is based on who is responsible for various control objectives, custody of assets, authorization, and record keeping. If the same individual is responsible for multiple, conflicting functions, such as authorization and custody of assets, then this is a potential control weakness and should be documented.
- Completing a risk assessment of the business process is required. The Risk Assessment is based on the question, 'what could go wrong?' or could a mistake occur through either intentionally or accidentally that would cause a misstatement to the Financial Statements to occur and go undetected. In addition, there are other risks in terms of fraud that should be part of the risk assessment.
- Each step in the process may have one or more risk statements associated with it. It is best practice to associate each risk statement to a type of risk. A representative list of business risks types for this purpose include:
    - business risk
    - financial risk
    - organizational risk
    - fraud risk
    - valuation risk
    - systems risk
- Every step in the process with a risk statement needs to have a least one control documented. It is possible to have multiple controls, also known as complimentary controls, for each risk statement. In this case, the control prevents the risk from occurring and going undetected. Many of the steps documented in the business process will serve as the basis for documenting the control. Evaluate the risk statements when documenting the control statement, so as to ensure the risk is properly controlled.

- Control Types are associated with the control statements and used to enhance the understanding of the control. The combination of different types of control types becomes the basis for Management's assessment of the overall control environment. In some cases, these control types are not mutually exclusive and can overlap each other. A representative list of control types include:
    - **Preventative** – prevents the risk from occurring (eg an order can not be generated if the customer has exceeded their credit limit)
    - **Detective** – the risk is still possible, but it can easily be detected (eg reconciliation of account balances to the general ledger)
    - **Automated** – controls developed into the IT system that will automatically execute and repeat without manual intervention. These may be scheduled to execute in the background process automatically (eg system process that automatically closes out invoices for payment after receipt is made and matched to the invoice)
    - **Manual** - relies on an individual or individuals to complete a control activity or step (eg comparing control totals to a batch total)
    - **Application** – similar to automated, but is configured into the software application which controls how the business process operates (eg online matching of invoices, receipts, and purchase orders during accounts payable invoice entry)
    - **IT dependent** – control based on the effectiveness of the IT control environment (eg system produced report that a manager reviews)

Control types become very useful to the development of the plan for testing the operating control effectiveness.

- Preventative controls and automated controls tend to be stronger and have more reliance placed on them. Conversely, a larger number of manual and detective controls would have less reliance and require more substantive testing to form management's assessment of the ICOFR. Generally, the more frequently a manual control operates, the more operations of the control the auditor needs to test.
- Controls that are relatively more important should be tested more extensively. For example, some controls may address multiple financial statement assertions, and certain period-end detective controls might be considered more important than related preventive controls.

- After completing the control types, additional information needs included with each control:
  - **Frequency** – daily, monthly, weekly, annually etc.
  - **Effective Date** – date when the control was implemented; this is most important in the case of a new control implemented during the course of the fiscal year

As in the case of control types, this information is needed when developing the plan for testing controls.

- The Risk and Control Matrix (R&CM) is the document used to summarize all the significant information needed to meet the Section 404 requirements. This document is rather straight forward to create, with the completion of the business process, risk assessments and control statements. Most companies use spreadsheet software when creating their R&CM. (See Appendix D – R&CM.) Key points include:
  - each activity/step in the process is documented and numbered
  - assign control numbers for each control statement as it will be used later for tracking during testing, remediation, and management reporting
- Key Controls are controls that management relies on when making an assessment of its Internal Control Over Financial Reporting (ICOFR). These are the only controls which are tested during the testing of operational effectiveness. All controls remain documented in the R&CM even if they are not identify as 'Key Controls' because they are part of the overall control environment and may mitigate other, non-financial risks. Non-Key controls may need to take a stronger role once testing and remediation takes place. Each key control should be identified within the R&CM.
- Additional best practices when identifying key controls:
  - make sure that all significant accounts and financial statement (FS) assertions are covered by at least one key control
  - consider the control type when determining key controls; an over-reliance on detective and manual controls could provide less assurance of overall control effectiveness during management's assessment
- Following completion of all documentation, including the flowcharts, narratives, SOD and RCM, each one should be signed off by the process owner. This ensures that the process owner agrees that the documentation is accurate and complete. Insuring the co-operation of process owners is crucial to the success of the project.

WALKTHROUGH (TEST OF CONTROL DESIGN)

Internal control over financial reporting is effectively designed when the controls complied with would be expected to prevent or detect errors or fraud that could result in material misstatements in the financial statements. A test of the design of controls, performed as a 'walkthrough' by an independent auditor helps determine whether the company has sufficient controls to meet the objectives of the Section 404 requirements.

- Tests of design can determine whether controls are designed effectively in support of the ICOFR control objectives. Tests of design are usually performed by inquiry and validating observation or inspection of documents, such as reports and completed forms; through screen prints; or most effectively by performing a process 'walkthrough'. A walkthrough is also known as 'Test of One', since sample sizes are not considered.
- Although walkthroughs are not required, a representative list of benefits includes:
  - confirm an understanding of the flow of a transaction
  - confirm an understanding of the design of controls, including those related to the prevention and detection of fraud
  - confirm an understanding of the complete process
  - evaluate the effectiveness of the design of controls
  - aid in the development of test procedures
- If, as a result of the process walkthrough, it is determined that controls were not designed to operate effectively, they must be remediated before testing of operating effectiveness can take place.

TESTING OF OPERATING EFFECTIVENESS

While the **Test of Design** establishes how the control should function, the **Test of Operating** effectiveness establishes how well the control actually operates over a time period. An independent auditor should evaluate the operating effectiveness of a control by determining whether the control is operating as designed, and whether the person performing the control possesses the necessary authority and qualifications to perform the control effectively. The auditor's testing of the operating effectiveness of such controls should occur at the time that the controls are operating.

- A test plan must be developed in order to schedule tests to be conducted in intervals that give reasonable assurance that controls are being performed in a consistent manner throughout the year, and not just at 'audit time'.

- In developing a test plan, start by creating a 'Summary of Key Controls Worksheet' by including only the Key Controls from the RCM. The Risk Control Matrix will be the basis for the test plan, as only key controls are tested.
- Develop detailed test procedures to include:
  - evidence needed
  - sample sizes
  - person responsible
  - source of testing
  - attributes tested

Attributes support all defined procedures within the control. For example, testing the control 'employee's access rights are removed timely from the system upon termination', the following attributes should be evaluated:
  - employee was removed from the system – Y/N
  - employee was removed timely – Y/N

In this case, the control test would fail even if all employees were removed from the system, but were completed six months after they left the firm.

- Once test procedures are developed, prepare a test lead sheet (see Appendix E – Test Lead Sheet) for each control test. This includes all details of the test, final conclusions regarding whether the control passes the test or not; and cross-references to the test evidence. Test evidence is usually attached as a separate document or noted as a work paper reference along with the control number noted in the Risk and Control Matrix.
- All test lead sheets are signed off by the auditor who performed the test, and by the management representative who reviewed and agreed with the conclusions.
- All test lead sheets and test evidence become part of the company's permanent record for SOX compliance. Therefore, a process for gathering and storing test results should be put in place. It is becoming more common today to store all documentation online in a centrally managed repository. Scanning test documents and evidence into electronic form provides a good solution for storage of documents.
- Companies should begin testing as early as possible, and make sure that every control is tested at least once by the end of the ninth month of the fiscal year. This will allow adequate time to remediate and re-test any ineffective controls before the final report is issued.

- Testing should continue as late in the year as possible to ensure that the results are representative of the entire fiscal year, and not only a portion of the year.
- If internal resources are used to complete management testing, the individual selected to conduct a test should not be the same person who performs the control. However, the person who performs the control should review the completed test work papers to validate accuracy.
- Deadlines for completing specific tests should be included in the plan. These deadlines should coincide with periodic update reports to the audit committee and management.
- When determining sample sizes, it is important to consider the frequency of the control. The following is a representative best practice guideline in the determination of sample sizes:
  - Annual Control – 1
  - Quarterly – 2 – 3
  - Monthly – 2 – 4
  - Weekly – 5 – 10
  - Daily – 15 – 30
  - Recurring * – 30 – 60

Multiple times per day

- The number of samples selected for each test should statistically provide adequate assurance that an accurate snapshot of normal operations is obtained.
- The test plan and samples sizes should be agreed upon with the external audit firm prior to starting the testing since each firm may have defined their own sample sizes.
- Samples should be randomly selected and should present a fair representation of the population of data.
- Wherever possible, samples should come directly from the original system of record, as opposed to ones that are manually prepared.
- Prior to requesting test evidence, obtain and review all related policies and procedures. Evidence should be collected from the person who performs the control. While collecting evidence, ask them to explain the control process. This ensures that the process is understood prior to testing and that any deviations from procedure can be identified.
- Systems' generated reports, original source documents, screen prints and independent observation of someone performing the control are all valid sources of evidence used in testing.

- Testing of controls is pass/fail. In other words, either the evidence supports that the controls are functioning effectively or it does not. Controls that do not pass the test are noted as exceptions.
- If a control is being performed regularly and according to procedure, evidence and documentation should be quick and easy to obtain. Evidence that is difficult to obtain might indicate an exception.
- All control exceptions are maintained in a separate and controlled 'Summary of Control Deficiencies' file, which becomes the system of record for evaluating significance of control deficiencies. (See Results – Reporting Deficiencies below.) Once a control is noted as deficient, it will remain on this list even if it is determined that actions were taken to remediate the exception.
- Take time to understand the cause and results of exceptions by determining if the test objective was met. Could additional testing support a different conclusion that the exception is not representative of the total population? If so, extend testing and re-evaluate. If there are still exceptions, then it is noted as a control deficiency and added to the summary of control deficiencies document.
- Control weaknesses should be risk assessed to determine the level of materiality. Follow-up actions should be appropriate to the level of materiality.
- Re-test controls after allowing adequate time for remediation. Results should be noted in the 'Audit Exceptions' file with date of remediation, and reported to the audit committee, external auditors and management.
- The practitioner should be aware that even after all testing is complete, additional test procedures will be performed at the end of year. The goal is to determine if there have been any changes to the control environment since the last tests were completed. This is particularly relevant when there is a long lag between the time of the initial test and end of year.

RESULTS – REPORTING DEFICIENCIES
- All control deficiencies need to be evaluated for their significance and whether a misstatement to the annual or interim financial statements is likely to occur. The PCAOB has developed the following definitions for evaluating the significance of deficiencies:
    - **Control Deficiency** – remote likelihood that a potential misstatement to the annual and interim financial statements could be more than inconsequential

- **Significant Deficiency** – a remote likelihood that a potential misstatement to the annual and interim financial statements could be more than material
- **Material Weakness** – likelihood of more than inconsequential misstatement of the annual or interim financial statement is more than remote
- Evaluating deficiencies becomes an important part of management assessment of the Internal Controls Over Financial Reporting (ICOFR). This process is complex and requires a great deal of professional judgment and analytical interpretation in forming the conclusions. Management should rely on consultants and their external auditors when assessing the significance of control deficiencies. External auditors will form their own assessment as well.
- **Aggregating Control Deficiencies** – all control deficiencies are grouped together by significant accounts and FS disclosure levels. The pervasiveness of control deficiencies across the entity and the risk of error and susceptibility to fraud are further evaluated. Using the above criteria, any number of control deficiencies could be upgraded to significant deficiencies and a number of significant deficiencies could result in material weaknesses.
- There are a number of factors considered when aggregating deficiencies, including whether the significant deficiencies:
  - affect the same financial statement account or disclosure
  - impact a common assertion in a financial statement account or disclosure
- IT General Control (ITGC) objectives support manual controls, automated application controls and IT dependent controls that relate directly to significant accounts and assertions. ITGC deficiencies are evaluated in terms of their impact on the above named controls, but will not necessarily result in misstatements. If the IT General Controls are determined through testing to be 'ineffective', then auditors can not rely on them to support the controls. This will mean that additional substantive test procedures and larger samples sizes are needed to judge the effectiveness of the controls.
- There are some situations where an ITGC deficiency could be upgraded and reported as a material weakness. If, for example, an ITGC deficiency is classified as a 'Significant Deficiency' and has not been corrected over a reasonable period of time, and if it was determined that the pervasiveness

of the deficiency was significant, then one could conclude that there is a material weakness in the company's overall control environment.
- All control deficiencies must be communicated to management, the audit committee and Board of Directors (as applicable) in writing. This communication also needs to include deficiencies that were remediated prior to the 'as of date'. In order to maintain control of this communication process, the status of this communication should be recorded for each deficiency in the 'Summary of Control Deficiencies' file.
- Once issues are reported, and agreed upon by management, remediation plans should be put into place. A spreadsheet or system program should be used to track the issues that have been remediated, re-tested, and deemed no longer an issue. Some companies have programs that store all of their controls and the test results for the current year and past years (most programs are bought and customized for the company). These programs also generally allow tracking of issues, remediation, and remediation testing results to show when an issue has been cleared. Access to these systems should be restricted to appropriate individuals. Whether a spreadsheet or system program is used, it is important to track controls, issues, and remediation. The system should have the ability to track when changes are made and to know by whom.

REMEDIATION
- Remediation of control weaknesses can be accomplished by implementing one or more strategies:
  - changing the business process
  - changing the system
  - adding complimentary controls (second level of controls that are performed in conjunction with other controls)
  - adding compensating controls

These are additional control procedures to ensure the control objectives are met. For example, SOD violations in a business unit with few employees could be compensated by adding a management review process of the work completed.
- If management calls out a compensating control after a key control has been tested and found ineffective, the compensating control must be tested for design and operating effectiveness, with the specific risk in mind that the compensating control must now mitigate.

- Management should be cautious to call out one control to compensate for many key controls. If the control which compensates for many key controls is found through testing to be ineffective, the end result easily escalates it into a significant deficiency.
- Monitoring controls by a senior manager, either Vice President or Director level, is viewed as a very effective compensating control when processes or staffing limitations prevent the control from functioning as designed.
- All supporting documentation, including the 'Summary of Control Deficiencies', needs to note the date the control was remediated. This will be referenced during year end and roll forward testing.

MANAGEMENT REPORTING
- Management is required to include its assessment of the effectiveness of the company's ICOFR in its annual report. Management's report on ICOFR must include the following:
    - a statement of Management's responsibility for establishing and maintaining adequate ICOFR for the company
    - a statement identifying the framework used by management to conduct the required assessment of the effectiveness of the company's ICOFR
    - an assessment of the effectiveness of the company's ICOFR as of the company's most recent fiscal year end, including an explicit statement as to whether that ICOFR is effective
    - a statement that the registered public accounting firm that audited financial statements included in the annual report has issued an attestation report on management's assessment of the company's ICOFR

IT GENERAL CONTROLS (ITGCs)
- ITGC are key to the ICOFR because they serve as the foundation for the effective functioning of controls throughout the organization and directly support the financial reporting process. As such, an integrated audit approach, with financial and IT auditors working closely together in the review of the ICOFR, is needed to meet the requirements of Section 404.

- In the same way that entity level controls are based on an established and well known control framework, IT control design should follow the same practice and adopt established and commonly-used frameworks. CoBiT®, ITIL®, and ISO17799 all meet these criteria and are the most commonly used for this purpose.
- Each of the above frameworks was created to satisfy different objectives; as such, the control objectives will vary from framework to framework. IT Management should carefully consider their internal technology environment and business requirements when developing their IT controls based on a particular framework.
- Section 404 considers only the information technology which directly supports the financial business processes, the number of controls and control objectives for SOX may be more limited that those needed to operate the business. For example, larger companies maintain a Disaster Recovery Plan, but it would not need to be absolutely defined as a control in order to complete SOX requirements. In addition, application software supporting non-financial processes (eg Customer Relationship Management (CRM)) may also not need to be reviewed for SOX.
- There are a minimum number of control objectives that need to be reviewed in order to satisfy the ITGC requirements of Section 404:
    - **Information System Planning** – IT is aligned with and supports the goals of the business
    - **Systems Development Life Cycle** – usually only comes into play when larger scale deployments of application software impacting the financial reporting process are made during the current year
    - **Program Change Control** – changes are authorized, approved and tested by someone other then the developer prior to moving into production
    - **Security Administration** – user access privileges are approved by user's manager prior to granting in system
    - **Operations** – system processes are managed, controlled and restricted to authorized personnel
    - **System Monitoring** – continuous monitoring of system performance and availability
- During the project planning phase, the technology environment supporting the financial reporting process was documented. This includes the following information:
    - application software

- host system operating system
- network operating system
- database
- telecommunications
- hardware platforms
- desktops

IT controls supporting the financial processes need to take all the different technology layers named above into consideration.

- Documenting the IT controls follows the same steps as the financial business processes. Narratives and flowcharts describing the process supporting the above name control objectives need completed and should follow the same standards of format and documentation.
- When obtaining evidence it is important that management relies on evidence produced directly from the system. For example, when reviewing password controls, the screen captures of the actual configuration should be used.
- An IT Risk and Control Matrix (R&CM) is prepared with similar information as a Financial R&CM, with risks, control objectives and controls, control types, key controls, effective dates, and frequency all documented. In addition, each control has defined needs to be associated with the supporting technology layer; application software, database, host-operating system and network operating system. For example, if the application software relies on password controls configured into the host operating system level, and not within the application software, then password controls would only need to be evaluated at the host operating system level.
- There are some unusual situations in which the above procedures are not sufficient for evaluating IT control. Additional techniques that may be used in evaluating these controls include:
  - **Benchmarking** – involves comparison of object libraries to determine dates of production moves of specific program objects; this may be used in situations where program change control cannot be relied on, and management needs to evaluate certain automated and application level controls
  - **Configuration of Application Controls** – many enterprise resource planning (ERP) packages have application controls configured into the system. A review of the configuration may be needed, to support how the application control is functioning

- **Source Code Reviews** – in rare cases where concerns regarding how certain complex functions support the control environment, a review of the program source code may be needed

It is important to note that, while the above techniques may, in rare cases be required, the technical nature of these techniques utilize resources with some very specific technical skills.

OUTSIDE PROCESSORS

- Many companies outsource financial applications and host systems to third party outside processors. Management however, is still responsible for the effectiveness of controls even when these processes are managed by another company. In this case, management must request a SAS70 report, prepared by an independent auditor, when evaluating their own control environment.
- There are two types of SAS70 reports companies issue:
  - Type I – Review of the Effectiveness of the Design of Controls
  - Type II - Review of the Operating Effectiveness of Controls.

Type II includes detail testing of the controls and is the standard that should be used for all SEC filers.

- Management should review the reports to determine whether any additional procedures should be performed to support its assessment of significant controls. Management is responsible for maintaining and evaluating controls over the transfer of information to and from the service organization(s). This is described in the user controls section of the SAS70.
- A SAS70 report discloses the controls that the end user company is responsible for implementing. For example, a host system outsourced to a third party processor will often maintain control of system security, but will require that the end user company be responsible for completing certain procedures such as granting and terminating user access. In this case, management needs to ensure that user control procedures are disclosed in the SAS70 as user controls are evaluated and included in their internal control procedures.
- If SAS70 is not available from a host company, then management needs to form their own assessment of the outside processor's controls. This requires that internal audit and/or external auditor review procedures at the location and form their own assessment.

- Management should determine whether third party processor's management has identified any changes in the service organization's controls subsequent to the period covered by the service auditor's report. These may include:
    - changes communicated by the service organization to management
    - changes in service organization personnel with whom management interacts
    - changes in reports or other data received from the service organization
    - changes in contracts or service-level agreements with the service organization
    - an error in the service organization's processing

Section 405 – Exemption
Domain: Accountability
Knowledge Area: Accounting and Finance
SOX Process: Planning

Section 405 Synopsis
Investment companies registered under Section 8 of the Investment Company Act of 1940 are exempted from requirements identified within Sections 401, 402 and 404.

Investment companies are defined as companies, including mutual funds, that engage primarily in investing, reinvesting, and trading in securities, and whose own securities are offered to the investing public.

Section 405 GASP
Companies that are exempt from the requirements of Sections 401, 402 and 404 should be aware that they must still comply with the requirements of Section 302. (See Section 302.)

Section 406 – Code of Ethics for Senior Financial Officers
Domain: Responsibility, Accountability
Knowledge Area: Accounting and Finance, Law, Ethics and Compliance
SOX Process: Reporting and Communication, Evaluation

Section 406 Synopsis

This section requires that a code of ethics for the CEO, CFO and senior accounting personnel should be adopted by the issuer. If a code of ethics is not adopted, the reason for non-adoption must be disclosed to the SEC on Form 8-K annually.

'Code of ethics' is defined as standards to promote honest and ethical conduct, including the ethical handling of actual or apparent conflicts of interest between personal and professional relationships.

Section 406 GASP

- A formal code of ethics, which specifically addresses code of ethics issues from the financial officers, including CEO, CFO and senior accounting personnel, needs to be established and monitored, along with associated compliance processes and practices.
- A formal code of ethics needs to be established, with input by legal counsel, and signed by the CEO and CFO or senior financial officer acknowledging their agreement to abide by the principles of the code.
- Human resources or ethics committee should develop an ethics training course for all employees and retain documentation of employees who have completed the course.
- The issuer is required to disclose whether it has adopted a code of ethics that applies to the company's principal executive officer, principal financial officer, principal accounting officer or controller, or persons performing similar functions. A company disclosing that it has not adopted such a code must disclose this fact and explain why it has not done so. A company also will be required promptly to disclose amendments to, and waivers from, the code of ethics relating to any of those officers.
- The CFO or senior financial officer is responsible for annually reporting code of ethics compliance to the SEC using Form 8-K.

Section 407 – Disclosure of Audit Committee Financial Expert

Domain: Responsibility, Accountability
Knowledge Area: Accounting and Finance
SOX Process: Reporting and Communication, Evaluation

Section 407 Synopsis

At a minimum, a 'financial expert' needs to be included in the company's audit committee, and disclosed to the SEC along with the regular periodic reports. If no financial expert is a member of the audit committee, the company must disclose the reason for non-compliance.

Financial expert is defined as a person who has, through education and experience as a public accountant or auditor or a principal financial officer, comptroller, or principal accounting officer of an issuer, or from a position involving the performance of similar functions –
1. developed an understanding of generally accepted accounting principles and financial statements
2. experience in:
   a) the preparation or auditing of financial statements of generally comparable issuers
   b) the application of such principles in connection with the accounting for estimates, accruals, and reserves
3. experience with internal accounting controls
4. developed an understanding of audit committee functions

Section 407 GASP

- The Board of Directors needs to recruit individual(s) with financial reporting and auditing expertise for service on the audit committee.
- The CFO must ensure that information about audit committee members has been disclosed to the SEC. The issuer is required to disclose whether it has at least one 'audit committee financial expert' serving on its audit committee, and if so, provide the name of the expert and whether the expert is independent of management. A company that does not have an audit committee financial expert must disclose this fact and explain why it has no such expert.
- Issuers are required to disclose the following:
  - the number and names of persons that the board of directors has determined to be the financial experts serving on the company's audit committee
  - whether the financial expert or experts are 'independent' and if not, an explanation of why they are not
  - whether the company has a financial expert serving on its audit committee at all, and if not, why not

- Issuing companies must disclose the information required of its financial expert in their periodic reports and to include the new disclosure in their annual reports on Form 10-K. The company should include this information with the election of directors, if the company voluntarily chooses to include this information in its proxy or information statement, and should file such statement with the SEC no later than 120 days after the end of the fiscal year covered by the Form 10-K.

Section 408 – Enhanced Review of Periodic Disclosures by Issuers

Domain: Governance
Knowledge Area: Accounting and Finance
SOX Process: Evaluation

Section 408 Synopsis

The SEC has the right to review financial statements and disclosures at their discretion, and is required to review these reports no less than once every three years.

The following factors may influence the frequency or scheduling of the reviews:
- material restatements of financial results
- significant volatility in issuer's stock price as compared to other issuers
- largest market capitalization
- emerging companies with disparities in price to earning ratios
- operations that significantly affect any material sector of the economy
- other factors that the Commission may consider relevant

Section 408 GASP

- Accounting and financial management should be aware that the SEC will periodically conduct a review of issuer's financial statements no less than once every three years.
- Accounting and financial management should allocate resources to review, respond to and provide additional information as necessary during the SEC review.
- Companies who report under Section 13(a) of the Securities Exchange Act of 1934, including filers of Form 10-K, are subject to review.

- Section 408 explicitly states the rights of the SEC to review financial records at their own discretion (minimally once every three years), and therefore companies in preparation for this requirement need to establish document and record management programs. In order to meet these sections of the law - the company must maintain the systematic control of records throughout their lifecycle from creation/receipt, use/circulation, and maintenance to disposition. Management needs to ensure that a working solution including an archived document and records management program is available and accessible when requested by the SEC.

Section 409 – Real Time Issuers Disclosures
Domain: Transparency
Knowledge Area: Accounting and Finance
SOX Process: Reporting and Communication

Section 409 Synopsis
Issuers are responsible for quickly disclosing information about material changes in the financial conditions or operations to the public.

Section 409 GASP
- It is management's responsibility to identify material changes on a real-time basis.
- The SEC has expanded its disclosure requirements and set an accelerated filing deadline for Form 8-Ks, used to report material events. The new SEC rules require that companies file Form 8-Ks within four business days of the event (the old requirement was five business days, or 15 calendar days). The industry standard for reporting material events is 24 to 48 hours, and some established SEC, New York Stock Exchange and NASDAQ rules mandate even shorter timelines for some events.
- Financial reporting personnel need to establish processes and procedures for disclosing information about material changes to the public within 48 hours (eg many companies use their public website as the way to disclose information to the public about material changes).
- Material change disclosures should be presented in a manner that is easy to read and understand for the general public, and can include graphs, charts and visual presentation aides.

CHAPTER 5:
Analyst Conflict of Interest

Practitioners Perspective and Regulation Synopsis

This Title in the Sarbanes-Oxley Act is a combination of independence, conflict of interest, and the concept of protection similar to the 'Whistleblower' of Title VIII, all rolled into one Title. It applies specifically to security analysts or those individuals chartered with publishing research on securities being offered to the public. Sarbanes-Oxley directed a registered securities association or national securities exchange (eg the Securities and Exchange Commission (SEC)), to modify their rules to protect analysts from aggressive brokers, should they have to issue a negative opinion. Under SOX, these analysts are protected from persecution by personnel in their own brokerage who might have an interest in a more favorable finding that would support their marketing efforts. Research has shown that the various exchanges, having one year from passage of this Title to conform, have participated with certain rule changes and amendments to be in compliance with the requirements of Sarbanes-Oxley and to provide more independence and protection for the analysts.

Regulation Text

SEC. 501. TREATMENT OF SECURITIES ANALYSTS BY REGISTERED SECURITIES ASSOCIATIONS AND NATIONAL SECURITIES EXCHANGES.
(a) RULES REGARDING SECURITIES ANALYSTS.—The Securities Exchange Act of 1934 (15 U.S.C. 78a et seq.) is amended by inserting after section 15C the following new section:

SEC. 15D. SECURITIES ANALYSTS AND RESEARCH REPORTS.

(a) ANALYST PROTECTIONS.—The Commission, or upon the authorization and direction of the Commission, a registered securities association or national securities exchange, shall have adopted, not later than 1 year after the date of enactment of this section, rules reasonably designed to address conflicts of interest that can arise when securities analysts recommend equity securities in research reports and public appearances, in order to improve the objectivity of research and provide investors with more useful and reliable information, including rules designed—

    (1) to foster greater public confidence in securities research, and to protect the objectivity and independence of securities analysts, by—

        (A) restricting the prepublication clearance or approval of research reports by persons employed by the broker or dealer who are engaged in investment banking activities, or persons not directly responsible for investment research, other than legal or compliance staff;

        (B) limiting the supervision and compensatory evaluation of securities analysts to officials employed by the broker or dealer who are not engaged in investment banking activities; and

        (C) requiring that a broker or dealer and persons employed by a broker or dealer who are involved with investment banking activities may not, directly or indirectly, retaliate against or threaten to retaliate against any securities analyst employed by that broker or dealer or its affiliates as a result of an adverse, negative, or otherwise unfavorable research report that may adversely affect the present or prospective investment banking relationship of the broker or dealer with the issuer that is the subject of the research report, except that such rules may not limit the authority of a broker or dealer to discipline a securities analyst for causes other than such research report in accordance with the policies and procedures of the firm;

    (2) to define periods during which brokers or dealers who have participated, or are to participate, in a public offering of securities as underwriters or dealers should not publish or otherwise distribute research reports relating to such securities or to the issuer of such securities;

(3) to establish structural and institutional safeguards within registered brokers or dealers to assure that securities analysts are separated by appropriate informational partitions within the firm from the review, pressure, or oversight of those whose involvement in investment banking activities might potentially bias their judgment or supervision; and

(4) to address such other issues as the Commission, or such association or exchange, determines appropriate.

(b) DISCLOSURE.—The Commission, or upon the authorization and direction of the Commission, a registered securities association or national securities exchange, shall have adopted, not later than 1 year after the date of enactment of this section, rules reasonably designed to require each securities analyst to disclose in public appearances, and each registered broker or dealer to disclose in each research report, as applicable, conflicts of interest that are known or should have been known by the securities analyst or the broker or dealer, to exist at the time of the appearance or the date of distribution of the report, including—

(1) the extent to which the securities analyst has debt or equity investments in the issuer that is the subject of the appearance or research report;

(2) whether any compensation has been received by the registered broker or dealer, or any affiliate thereof, including the securities analyst, from the issuer that is the subject of the appearance or research report, subject to such exemptions as the Commission may determine appropriate and necessary to prevent disclosure by virtue of this paragraph of material non-public information regarding specific potential future investment banking transactions of such issuer, as is appropriate in the public interest and consistent with the protection of investors;

(3) whether an issuer, the securities of which are recommended in the appearance or research report, currently is, or during the 1-year period preceding the date of the appearance or date of distribution of the report has been, a client of the registered broker or dealer, and if so, stating the types of services provided to the issuer;

(4) whether the securities analyst received compensation with respect to a research report, based upon (among any other factors) the investment banking revenues (either generally or specifically earned from the issuer being analyzed) of the registered broker or dealer; and

(5) such other disclosures of conflicts of interest that are material to investors, research analysts, or the broker or dealer as the Commission, or such association or exchange, determines appropriate.

(c) DEFINITIONS.—In this section—
(1) the term 'securities analyst' means any associated person of a registered broker or dealer that is principally responsible for, and any associated person who reports directly or indirectly to a securities analyst in connection with, the preparation of the substance of a research report, whether or not any such person has the job title of 'securities analyst'; and
(2) the term 'research report' means a written or electronic communication that includes an analysis of equity securities of individual companies or industries, and that provides information reasonably sufficient upon which to base an investment decision."

(b) ENFORCEMENT—Section 21B (a) of the Securities Exchange Act of 1934 (15 U.S.C. 78u–2(a)) is amended by inserting "15D," before "15B".

(c) COMMISSION AUTHORITY—The Commission may promulgate and amend its regulations, or direct a registered securities association or national securities exchange to promulgate and amend its rules, to carry out section 15D of the Securities Exchange Act of 1934, as added by this section, as is necessary for the protection of investors and in the public interest.

Section 501 - Treatment of Securities Analysts by Registered Securities Associations and National Securities Exchanges

Domain: Responsibility, Accountability
Knowledge Area: Law, Ethics and Compliance
SOX Process: Independence

Section 501 Synopsis
- This Title directs registered securities association or national securities exchanges (eg the National Association of Securities Dealers (NASD)) to modify their rules to protect analysts in support of more independent and objective findings through their own means within one year from passage of the Title.

- Another aim of this Title to the SOX Act is to insulate or make more independent the analysts of a public offering from those promoting investments in that security, even if the primary underwriter of the security is the same firm employing the analyst.

Section 501 GASP

If there are any concerns whether the securities analysts are independent and objective, then the public should make sure the particular exchange in which the analyst participates has modified their rules according to this SOX Title. This can be done by checking the latest rulings posted on the website of the particular exchange in which you participate. As an example – the National Association of Securities Dealers (NASD) posted their announcement of conformance with the following link - http://nasd.complinet.com/file_store/pdf/rulebooks/nasd_0344.pdf

CHAPTER 6:
Commission Resources and Authority

Practitioners Perspective and Regulation Synopsis
Title VI addresses amendments to prior legislation regarding the authorized appropriations for the Securities Exchange Commission's activities, the Federal Court's ability to impose penny stock bars, and the Commission's authority over professionals, including brokers, dealers, issuers, auditors, and attorneys practicing before the Commission.

Generally Accepted SOX Practice
There are no generally accepted SOX practices that apply to this particular Title as it is the portion of the SOX Act that provides the funding, ongoing financial support and specific authorities for the Commission to conduct business. However, the practitioner should be constantly aware of any further changes as it could impact activities within the brokerage community or relationships with companies governed by other sections of the SOX Act.

Regulation Text

SEC. 601. AUTHORIZATION OF APPROPRIATIONS.
Section 35 of the Securities Exchange Act of 1934 (15 U.S.C. 78kk) is amended to read as follows:
SEC. 35. AUTHORIZATION OF APPROPRIATIONS.
In addition to any other funds authorized to be appropriated to the Commission, there are authorized to be appropriated to carry out the functions, powers, and duties of the Commission, $776,000,000 for fiscal year 2003, of which—

(1) $102,700,000 shall be available to fund additional compensation, including salaries and benefits, as authorized in the Investor and Capital Markets Fee Relief Act (Public Law 107–123; 115 Stat. 2390 et seq.);
(2) $108,400,000 shall be available for information technology, security enhancements, and recovery and mitigation activities in light of the terrorist attacks of September 11, 2001; and
(3) $98,000,000 shall be available to add not fewer than an additional 200 qualified professionals to provide enhanced oversight of auditors and audit services required by the Federal securities laws, and to improve Commission investigative and disciplinary efforts with respect to such auditors and services, as well as for additional professional support staff necessary to strengthen the programs of the Commission involving Full Disclosure and Prevention and Suppression of Fraud, risk management, industry technology review, compliance, inspections, examinations, market regulation, and investment management..

SEC. 602. APPEARANCE AND PRACTICE BEFORE THE COMMISSION.

The Securities Exchange Act of 1934 (15 U.S.C. 78a et seq.) is amended by inserting after section 4B the following:

SEC. 4C. APPEARANCE AND PRACTICE BEFORE THE COMMISSION.

(a) AUTHORITY TO CENSURE.—The Commission may censure any person, or deny, temporarily or permanently, to any person the privilege of appearing or practicing before the Commission in any way, if that person is found by the Commission, after notice and opportunity for hearing in the matter—
(1) not to possess the requisite qualifications to represent others;
(2) to be lacking in character or integrity, or to have engaged in unethical or improper professional conduct; or
(3) to have willfully violated, or willfully aided and abetted the violation of, any provision of the securities laws or the rules and regulations issued thereunder.
(b) DEFINITION.—With respect to any registered public accounting firm or associated person, for purposes of this section, the term 'improper professional conduct' means—

(1) intentional or knowing conduct, including reckless conduct, that results in a violation of applicable professional standards; and

(2) negligent conduct in the form of—

(A) a single instance of highly unreasonable conduct that results in a violation of applicable professional standards in circumstances in which the registered public accounting firm or associated person knows, or should know, that heightened scrutiny is warranted; or

(B) repeated instances of unreasonable conduct, each resulting in a violation of applicable professional standards, that indicate a lack of competence to practice before the Commission."

SEC. 603. FEDERAL COURT AUTHORITY TO IMPOSE PENNY STOCK BARS.

(a) SECURITIES EXCHANGE ACT OF 1934.—Section 21(d) of the Securities Exchange Act of 1934 (15 U.S.C. 78u(d)), as amended by this Act, is amended by adding at the end the following:

"(6) AUTHORITY OF A COURT TO PROHIBIT PERSONS FROM PARTICIPATING IN AN OFFERING OF PENNY STOCK.—

(A) IN GENERAL.—In any proceeding under paragraph (1) against any person participating in, or, at the time of the alleged misconduct who was participating in, an offering of penny stock, the court may prohibit that person from participating in an offering of penny stock, conditionally or unconditionally, and permanently or for such period of time as the court shall determine.

(B) DEFINITION.—For purposes of this paragraph, the term 'person participating in an offering of penny stock' includes any person engaging in activities with a broker, dealer, or issuer for purposes of issuing, trading, or inducing or attempting to induce the purchase or sale of, any penny stock. The Commission may, by rule or regulation, define such term to include other activities, and may, by rule, regulation, or order, exempt any person or class of persons, in whole or in part, conditionally or unconditionally, from inclusion in such term."

(b) SECURITIES ACT OF 1933.—Section 20 of the Securities Act of 1933 (15 U.S.C. 77t) is amended by adding at the end the following:
"(g) AUTHORITY OF A COURT TO PROHIBIT PERSONS FROM PARTICIPATING IN AN OFFERING OF PENNY STOCK.—

(1) IN GENERAL.—In any proceeding under subsection (a) against any person participating in, or, at the time of the alleged misconduct, who was participating in, an offering of penny stock, the court may prohibit that person from participating in an offering of penny stock, conditionally or unconditionally, and permanently or for such period of time as the court shall determine.

(2) DEFINITION.—For purposes of this subsection, the term 'person participating in an offering of penny stock' includes any person engaging in activities with a broker, dealer, or issuer for purposes of issuing, trading, or inducing or attempting to induce the purchase or sale of, any penny stock. The Commission may, by rule or regulation, define such term to include other activities, and may, by rule, regulation, or order, exempt any person or class of persons, in whole or in part, conditionally or unconditionally, from inclusion in such term."

SEC. 604. QUALIFICATIONS OF ASSOCIATED PERSONS OF BROKERS AND DEALERS.

(a) BROKERS AND DEALERS.—Section 15(b)(4) of the Securities Exchange Act of 1934 (15 U.S.C. 78o) is amended—

(1) by striking subparagraph (F) and inserting the following:

(F) is subject to any order of the Commission barring or suspending the right of the person to be associated with a broker or dealer;"; and

(2) in subparagraph

(G), by striking the period at the end and inserting the following: "; or (H) is subject to any final order of a State securities commission (or any agency or officer performing like functions), State authority that supervises or examines banks, savings associations, or credit unions, State insurance commission (or any agency or office performing like functions), an appropriate Federal banking agency (as defined in section 3 of the Federal Deposit Insurance Act (12 U.S.C. 1813(q))), or the National Credit Union Administration, that—

(i) bars such person from association with an entity regulated by such commission, authority, agency, or officer, or from engaging in the business of securities, Insurance, banking, savings association activities, or credit union activities; or

(ii) constitutes a final order based on violations of any laws or regulations that prohibit fraudulent, manipulative, or deceptive conduct."

(b) INVESTMENT ADVISERS.—Section 203(e) of the Investment Advisers Act of 1940 (15 U.S.C. 80b–3(e)) is amended—

(1) by striking paragraph (7) and inserting the following:

"(7) is subject to any order of the Commission barring or suspending the right of the person to be associated with an investment adviser;";

(2) in paragraph (8), by striking the period at the end and inserting "; or"; and

(3) by adding at the end the following:

"(9) is subject to any final order of a State securities commission (or any agency or officer performing like functions), State authority that supervises or examines banks, savings associations, or credit unions, State insurance commission (or any agency or office performing like functions), an appropriate Federal banking agency (as defined in section 3 of the Federal Deposit Insurance Act (12 U.S.C. 1813(q))), or the National Credit Union Administration, that—

"(A) bars such person from association with an entity regulated by such commission, authority, agency, or officer, or from engaging in the business of securities, insurance, banking, savings association activities, or credit union activities; or

"(B) constitutes a final order based on violations of any laws or regulations that prohibit fraudulent, manipulative, or deceptive conduct."

(c) CONFORMING AMENDMENTS.—

(1) SECURITIES EXCHANGE ACT OF 1934.—The Securities Exchange Act of 1934 (15 U.S.C. 78a et seq.) is amended—

(A) in section 3(a)(39)(F) (15 U.S.C. 78c(a)(39)(F))—

(i) by striking "or (G)" and inserting "(H), or (G)"; and

(ii) by inserting ", or is subject to an order or finding," before "enumerated";

(B) in each of section 15(b)(6)(A)(i) (15 U.S.C. 78o(b)(6)(A)(i)), paragraphs (2) and (4) of section 15B(c) (15 U.S.C. 78o-4(c)), and subparagraphs (A) and (C) of section 15C(c)(1) (15 U.S.C. 78o-5(c)(1))—

   (i) by striking "or (G)" each place that term appears and inserting "(H), or (G)"; and

   (ii) by striking "or omission" each place that term appears, and inserting ", or is subject to an order or finding,"; and

(C) in each of paragraphs (3)(A) and (4)(C) of section 17A(c) (15 U.S.C. 78q-1(c))—

   (i) by striking "or (G)" each place that term appears and inserting "(H), or (G)"; and

   (ii) by inserting ", or is subject to an order or finding," before "enumerated" each place that term appears.

(2) INVESTMENT ADVISERS ACT OF 1940.—Section 203(f) of the Investment Advisers Act of 1940 (15 U.S.C. 80b-3(f)) is amended—

   (A) by striking "or (8)" and inserting "(8), or (9)"; and

   (B) by inserting "or (3)" after "paragraph (2)".

Section 601 – Authorizations of Appropriations

Domain: Governance
Knowledge Area: Law, Ethics and Compliance
SOX Process: Audit, Compliance and Enforcement

Section 601 Synopsis

This section amends the Securities Exchange Act of 1934; the amount of funds appropriated to the Commission to carry out the increased duties in 2003. Areas of increase included:
- staff compensation
- information technology
- security enhancements due to September 11th terrorist attacks

Additional appropriations include:
- increased oversight of audit services
- new federal securities laws requirements
- at least 200 additional staff positions to increase fraud prevention and risk management

Section 601 GASP
Not Applicable.

Section 602 – Appearance and Practice before the Commission
Domain: Governance
Knowledge Area: Law, Ethics and Compliance
SOX Process: Audit, Compliance and Enforcement

Section 602 Synopsis
The SEC has the authority to refuse or reject any auditor as follows:
- lacks the required qualification to represent others
- lacks integrity
- has violated federal securities laws

Section 602 GASP
Not Applicable.

Section 603 – Federal Court Authority to Impose Penny Stock Bars
Domain: Governance
Knowledge Area: Law, Ethics and Compliance
SOX Process: Audit, Compliance and Enforcement

Section 603 Synopsis
This section amends the Securities Exchange Act of 1934 and also the Securities Act of 1933 by granting federal courts the ability to prohibit specified brokers, dealers, and issuers from participating in penny stock transactions.

Section 603 GASP
Not Applicable.

Section 604 – Associated Persons of Brokers and Dealers
Domain: Governance
Knowledge Area: Law, Ethics and Compliance
SOX Process: Audit, Compliance and Enforcement

Section 604 - Qualifications of Associated Persons of Brokers and Dealers

This section amends the Securities Exchange Act of 1934 and the Investment Advisors Act of 1940 by granting the Commission the ability to censure or restrict an associated person or a broker or a dealer from engaging in the business of securities, banking, or insurance.

Section 604 GASP

Not Applicable.

CHAPTER 7:
Studies and Reports

Practitioners Perspective and Regulation Synopsis

Title XII of the SOX mandates that the General Accounting Office (GAO) and the Securities and Exchange Commission study and report findings on the root causes of the various financial crises leading to public mistrust of Wall Street and corporate America that occurred in the late 1990s and early 2000.

Specifically, Title VII required that the following studies be issued:
- the consolidation of public accounting firms since 1989; analyze the past, present and future impact of the consolidations, and create solutions to problems discovered to be caused by such consolidations
- the role and function of credit rating agencies in the operation of the securities market
- the number of securities professionals (public accountants, investment bankers, attorneys) who have been found to have aided and abetted a violation of securities law and who have not been disciplined
- enforcement actions by the SEC regarding re-statements, violations of reporting requirements, and other violations, for the five year period prior to the date the SOX Act was passed
- whether investment banks and financial advisers assisted public companies in manipulating their earnings (specifically Enron and WorldCom)

The studies have been comprehensive, with action plans assigned going forward. To date, some of the action plans have been finalized and are considered policy, while others are still ongoing.

Regulation Text

SEC. 701. GAO STUDY AND REPORT REGARDING CONSOLIDATION OF PUBLIC ACCOUNTING FIRMS.

(a) STUDY REQUIRED.—The Comptroller General of the United States shall conduct a study—
    (1) to identify—
        (A) the factors that have led to the consolidation of public accounting firms since 1989 and the consequent reduction in the number of firms capable of providing audit services to large national and multi-national business organizations that are subject to the securities laws;
        (B) the present and future impact of the condition described in subparagraph (A) on capital formation and securities markets, both domestic and international; and
        (C) solutions to any problems identified under subparagraph (B), including ways to increase competition and the number of firms capable of providing audit services to large national and multinational business organizations that are subject to the securities laws;
    (2) of the problems, if any, faced by business organizations that have resulted from limited competition among public accounting firms, including—
        (A) higher costs;
        (B) lower quality of services;
        (C) impairment of auditor independence; or
        (D) lack of choice; and
    (3) whether and to what extent Federal or State regulations impede competition among public accounting firms.

(b) CONSULTATION.—In planning and conducting the study under this section, the Comptroller General shall consult with—
    (1) the Commission;
    (2) the regulatory agencies that perform functions similar to the Commission within the other member countries of the Group of Seven Industrialized Nations;
    (3) the Department of Justice; and
    (4) any other public or private sector organization that the Comptroller General considers appropriate.

(c) REPORT REQUIRED.—Not later than 1 year after the date of enactment of this Act, the Comptroller General shall submit a report on the results of the study required by this section to the Committee on Banking, Housing, and Urban Affairs of the Senate and the Committee on Financial Services of the House of Representatives.

SEC. 702. COMMISSION STUDY AND REPORT REGARDING CREDIT RATING AGENCIES.

(a) STUDY REQUIRED.—

(1) IN GENERAL.—The Commission shall conduct a study of the role and function of credit rating agencies in the operation of the securities market.

(2) AREAS OF CONSIDERATION.—The study required by this subsection shall examine—

(A) the role of credit rating agencies in the evaluation of issuers of securities;

(B) the importance of that role to investors and the functioning of the securities markets;

(C) any impediments to the accurate appraisal by credit rating agencies of the financial resources and risks of issuers of securities;

(D) any barriers to entry into the business of acting as a credit rating agency, and any measures needed to remove such barriers;

(E) any measures which may be required to improve the dissemination of information concerning such resources and risks when credit rating agencies announce credit ratings; and

(F) any conflicts of interest in the operation of credit rating agencies and measures to prevent such conflicts or ameliorate the consequences of such conflicts.

(b) REPORT REQUIRED.—The Commission shall submit a report on the study required by subsection (a) to the President, the Committee on Financial Services of the House of Representatives, and the Committee on Banking, Housing, and Urban Affairs of the Senate not later than 180 days after the date of enactment of this Act.

SEC. 703. STUDY AND REPORT ON VIOLATORS AND VIOLATIONS.

(a) STUDY.—The Commission shall conduct a study to determine, based upon information for the period from January 1, 1998, to December 31, 2001—

> (1) the number of securities professionals, defined as public accountants, public accounting firms, investment bankers, investment advisers, brokers, dealers, attorneys, and other securities professionals practicing before the Commission—
>> (A) who have been found to have aided and abetted a violation of the Federal securities laws, including rules or regulations promulgated thereunder (collectively referred to in this section as "Federal securities laws"), but who have not been sanctioned, disciplined, or otherwise penalized as a primary violator in any administrative action or civil proceeding, including in any settlement of such an action or proceeding (referred to in this section as "aiders and abettors"); and
>> (B) who have been found to have been primary violators of the Federal securities laws;
>
> (2) a description of the Federal securities laws violations committed by aiders and abettors and by primary violators, including—
>> (A) the specific provision of the Federal securities laws violated;
>> (B) the specific sanctions and penalties imposed upon such aiders and abettors and primary violators, including the amount of any monetary penalties assessed upon and collected from such persons;
>> (C) the occurrence of multiple violations by the same person or persons, either as an aider or abettor or as a primary violator; and
>> D) whether, as to each such violator, disciplinary sanctions have been imposed, including any censure, suspension, temporary bar, or permanent bar to practice before the Commission; and
>
> (3) the amount of disgorgement, restitution, or any other fines or payments that the Commission has assessed upon and collected from, aiders and abettors and from primary violators.

(b) REPORT.—A report based upon the study conducted pursuant to subsection (a) shall be submitted to the Committee on Banking, Housing, and Urban Affairs of the Senate, and the Committee on Financial Services of the House of Representatives not later than 6 months after the date of enactment of this Act.

SEC. 704. STUDY OF ENFORCEMENT ACTIONS.

(a) STUDY REQUIRED.—The Commission shall review and analyze all enforcement actions by the Commission involving violations of reporting requirements imposed under the securities laws, and restatements of financial statements, over the 5-year period preceding the date of enactment of this Act, to identify areas of reporting that are most susceptible to fraud, inappropriate manipulation, or inappropriate earnings management, such as revenue recognition and the accounting treatment of off-balance sheet special purpose entities.

(b) REPORT REQUIRED.—The Commission shall report its findings to the Committee on Financial Services of the House of Representatives and the Committee on Banking, Housing, and Urban Affairs of the Senate, not later than 180 days after the date of enactment of this Act, and shall use such findings to revise its rules and regulations, as necessary. The report shall include a discussion of regulatory or legislative steps that are recommended or that may be necessary to address concerns identified in the study.

SEC. 705. STUDY OF INVESTMENT BANKS.

(a) GAO STUDY.—The Comptroller General of the United States shall conduct a study on whether investment banks and financial advisers assisted public companies in manipulating their earnings and obfuscating their true financial condition. The study should address the rule of investment banks and financial advisers—

(1) in the collapse of the Enron Corporation, including with respect to the design and implementation of derivatives transactions, transactions involving special purpose vehicles, and other financial arrangements that may have had the effect of altering the company's reported financial statements in ways that obscured the true financial picture of the company;

(2) in the failure of Global Crossing, including with respect to transactions involving swaps of fiberoptic cable capacity, in the designing transactions that may have had the effect of altering the company's reported financial statements in ways that obscured the true financial picture of the company; and

(3) generally, in creating and marketing transactions which may have been designed solely to enable companies to manipulate revenue streams, obtain loans, or move liabilities off balance sheets without altering the economic and business risks faced by the companies or any other mechanism to obscure a company's financial picture.

(b) REPORT.—The Comptroller General shall report to Congress not later than 180 days after the date of enactment of this Act on the results of the study required by this section. The report shall include a discussion of regulatory or legislative steps that are recommended or that may be necessary to address concerns identified in the study.

Section 701 – GAO Study and Report Regarding Consolidation of Public Accounting Firms

Domain: Governance
Knowledge Area: Law, Ethics and Compliance
SOX Process: Non-Applicable

Section 701 Synopsis

This section addresses the General Accounting Office (GAO) study concerning public accounting firms - 'Mandated Study on Consolidation and Competition' reported to the Senate Committee on Banking, Housing and Urban Affairs and The House Committee of Financial Services, July 2003.

The report was mandated in Section 701 of the SOX Act because the audit market for large public companies is an oligopoly, and the mergers among the largest firms in the 1980s and 1990s, and the dissolution of Arthur Anderson in 2002, significantly increased concentration among the largest firms, known as the 'Big 4'. These four firms currently audit over 78 per cent of all US public companies, and 99 per cent of all public company sales.

This consolidation and the resulting concentration have raised a number of concerns about the concentration of market power and the potential effect on competition, pricing, and various other factors, including audit quality and auditor independence.

To address these issues, the Sarbanes-Oxley Act of 2002 mandated that the GAO study the following:

- the factors contributing to the mergers of accounting firms
- the implications of consolidation on competition and client choice, audit fees; audit quality, and auditor independence
- the impact of consolidation on capital formation and securities markets
- barriers to entry faced by smaller accounting firms in competing with the largest firms for large public company audits

The report made no specific recommendations, but published the following results of the study:

- Consolidation of the largest public accounting firms was driven primarily by the need for three factors:
  - the need to deliver services globally to match the growing size and reach of public companies in an expanding global economy
  - the need to reduce costs by achieving greater economies of scale
  - the need for more industry-specific and technical expertise
- No empirical evidence was found that competition in the market for audit services was impaired to date.
- No research was found linking the impact of audit fees, audit quality, and auditor independence to consolidation of the industry. It was found that there were mixed views on these concerns (fees, quality, and independence), but it was viewed that, due to on-going changes in the market, past behavior may not be indicative of future behavior.
- No evidence suggested that consolidation of the accounting industry had directly impacted capital formation or securities markets.
- Finally, the report concluded that smaller accounting firms faced significant barriers to entry to the audit market for large, multinational public companies.

Section 701 GASP
Not Applicable.

Section 702 – Commission Study and Report Regarding Credit Rating Agencies

Domain: Governance
Knowledge Area: Law, Ethics and Compliance
SOX Process: Non-Applicable

Section 702 Synopsis

The Commission shall submit a report on the study required by subsection (a) to the President, the Committee on Financial Services of the House of Representatives, and the Committee on Banking, Housing, and Urban Affairs of the Senate, not later than 180 days after the date of enactment of this Act. Specifically 702(b): The report included analyzing the 6 areas of consideration required in Section 702(a) and was submitted January, 2003.

The report is designed to address each of the topics identified for Commission study in the Sarbanes-Oxley Act, including:
- the role of credit rating agencies and their importance to the securities markets
- impediments faced by credit rating agencies in performing that role
- measures to improve information flow to the market from rating agencies
- barriers to entry into the credit rating business
- conflicts of interest faced by rating agencies

The report called for by the Sarbanes-Oxley Act coincided with a review of credit rating agencies already underway at the Commission; the other report addresses certain issues regarding rating agencies, such as:
- allegations of anticompetitive or unfair practices
- the level of diligence of credit rating agencies
- the extent and manner of Commission oversight

The report identified a wide range of issues that deserve further study. Accordingly, the Commission planned to publish a concept release within 60 days of this report to address concerns related to credit rating agencies and expects to issue proposed rules, after reviewing and evaluating the comments received on the concept release, within a reasonable period of time after the close of the comment period. The issues to be studied by the Commission in more depth include the following:

Information Flow
- whether rating agencies should disclose more information about their ratings decisions
- whether there should be improvements to the extent and quality of disclosure by issuers (including disclosures relating to ratings triggers)

Potential Conflicts of Interest
- whether rating agencies should implement procedures to manage potential conflicts of interest that arise when issuers pay for ratings
- whether rating agencies should prohibit (or severely restrict) direct contacts between rating analysts and subscribers
- whether rating agencies should implement procedures to manage potential conflicts of interest that arise when rating agencies develop ancillary fee-based businesses

Alleged Anticompetitive or Unfair Practices
- the extent to which allegations of anticompetitive or unfair practices by large credit rating agencies have merit and, if so, possible Commission action to address them

Reducing Potential Regulatory Barriers to Entry
- whether the current regulatory recognition criteria for rating agencies should be clarified
- whether timing goals for the evaluation of applications for regulatory recognition should be instituted
- whether rating agencies that cover a limited sector of the debt market, or confine their activity to a limited geographic area, should be recognized for regulatory purposes
- whether there are viable alternatives to the recognition of rating agencies in Commission rules and regulations

Ongoing Oversight
- whether more direct, ongoing oversight of rating agencies is warranted and, if so, the appropriate means for doing so (and whether it is advisable to ask Congress for specific legislative oversight authority)
- whether rating agencies should incorporate general standards of diligence in performing their ratings analysis, and with respect to the training and qualifications of credit rating analysts

Section 702 GASP
Not Applicable.

Section 703 – Study and Report on Violators and Violations

Domain: Governance
Knowledge Area: Law, Ethics and Compliance
SOX Process: Non-Applicable

Section 703 Synopsis
Report of the Securities and Exchange Commission: Section 703 of the Sarbanes-Oxley Act of 2002 'Study and Report on Violations by Security Professionals' December 2002. The report included the number of securities professionals who have aided and abetted, or were primary violators of the federal securities laws in calendar years 1998, 1999, 2000 and 2001.

The report concluded its findings by issuing the following conclusions:
- During the four-year period of the study, 1,596 securities professionals were found to have aided and abetted violations of and/or violated the federal securities laws.
- Most of these securities professionals were charged solely as primary violators or as both primary violators, and aiders and abettors.
- Only 13 of these 1,596 securities professionals were charged solely as aiders and abettors.
- The most common type of securities professionals against whom the SEC brought actions were individuals associated with broker-dealers, such as registered representatives and branch managers.
- The most common types of cases involved securities offerings and fraud against broker-dealer customers.
- The most prevalent sanctions ordered were permanent injunctions, civil penalties, disgorgement, and bars from association with broker-dealers.
- The most frequently violated sections of the federal securities laws were the general anti-fraud provisions of the Securities Act and the Exchange Act.
- The most frequently violated sections of the federal securities laws were the anti-fraud provisions:
  - Section 10(b) of the Exchange Act of 1934 (965)
  - Section 17(a) of the Securities Act of 1933 (741)

- The next most frequently violated provisions involved violations of the securities registration provisions:
  - (Sections 5(a) and 5(c) of the Securities Act) (302 and 290, respectively)
  - broker-dealer registration provisions (Section 15(a) of the Exchange Act) (265)
- Securities professionals were much more likely to have been found principal violators (1,299) than aiders and abettors (13).
- Two hundred and eighty four (284) securities professionals were charged as both a principal violator, and an aider and abettor.

Section 703 GASP
Not Applicable.

Section 704 – Study of Enforcement Actions
Domain: Governance
Knowledge Area: Law, Ethics and Compliance
SOX Process: Non-Applicable

Section 704 Synopsis
Section 704 directed the SEC to study enforcement actions over the five years preceding its enactment, in order to identify areas of issuer financial reporting that are most susceptible to fraud, inappropriate manipulation or inappropriate earnings management (the 'Study'). In addition, Section 704 directed the SEC to report its findings to Congress, including a discussion of recommended regulation or legislation (the 'Report'). This Study involved the review of all of the Commission's enforcement actions filed during the period July 31, 1997 through July 30, 2002 (the 'Study period') that were based on improper issuer financial reporting, fraud, audit failure, or auditor independence violations.

Section 704 directs the Commission to include in this Report a discussion of recommended steps to address concerns identified by this Study. The Sarbanes-Oxley Act provides numerous provisions, including the creation of the Public Company Accounting Oversight Board, which were designed to address many of the concerns identified in this Report. This Report contains a few recommendations for additional reforms primarily designed to aid the Commission in enforcing the federal securities laws in the

financial reporting and issuer disclosure area. Specifically, the Commission recommends addressing two areas of issuer disclosure: the uniform reporting of restatements of financial statements, and improved MD&A disclosure. In addition, based on this Report, the Commission recommends the enactment of legislation to:
- allow companies to produce internal reports and other documents pertaining to investigations without waiving any privileges
- provide access by Commission staff to grand jury materials
- provide for nationwide service of process for testimony in Commission litigation

Results of Study - Areas of Reporting Most Susceptible to Fraud

The Study identified several areas of reporting in the 227 enforcement matters reviewed that have been susceptible to fraud and other improper conduct:
- improper revenue recognition
- improper expense recognition
- improper accounting in connection with business combinations
- 'other' conduct, including:
  - inadequate disclosures in Management Discussion and Analysis ('MD&A') and elsewhere in issuer filings
  - failure to disclose related party transactions
  - inappropriate accounting for non-monetary and round-trip transactions
  - improper accounting for foreign payments in violation of the Foreign Corrupt Practices Act ('FCPA')
  - improper use of off-balance sheet arrangements
  - improper use of non-GAAP financial measures

Section 704 GASP

The Chief Financial Officer and/or Audit Committee should carefully review the findings of this report with respect to areas most likely to be susceptible to fraud. (See Appendix.) Accordingly, the companies internal control environment should, at a minimum, develop responses to address and reduce the likelihood of each of the fraud possibilities listed. This could be done in the form of corporate policies, segregation of duties and design of controls.

Section 705 - Study of Investment Banks

Domain: Governance
Knowledge Area: Law, Ethics and Compliance
SOX Process: Non-Applicable

Section 705 Synopsis:

The United States General Accounting Office-Investment Banks, 'The Role of Firms and Their Analysts with Enron and Global Crossing' March 2003. Highlights of GAO-03-511- 'Why GAO Did This Study'

In the wake of a series of recent corporate scandals and bankruptcies, the Sarbanes-Oxley Act mandated that GAO study the involvement of investment banks with two companies, Enron and Global Crossing. In this report, the term 'investment bank' includes not only securities firms, but also those bank holding companies with securities affiliates or business divisions that assist clients in obtaining funds to finance investment projects. Since the activities identified in this report are the subject of ongoing and extensive investigations and litigation by competent authorities, it is not GAO's role to determine the propriety of any of the parties' activities. To help the Congress better understand the activities of investment banks with respect to these companies GAO agreed to provide publicly available information on the roles of investment banks played in designing, executing and participating in certain structured finance transactions, investment banks' and federal regulators' oversight of these transactions, and the role that the banks' research analysts played with Enron and Global Crossing.

Certain investment banks facilitated and participated in complex financial transactions with Enron, despite allegedly knowing that the intent of the transactions was to manipulate and obscure Enron's true financial condition. The investment banks involved in the transactions we reviewed contended that their actions were appropriate and that Enron had not revealed its true purpose in obtaining their assistance. While investment banks are not responsible for the financial reporting of their clients, if it is proven that the investment banks knowingly assisted Enron in engaging in securities law violations, SEC has the authority to take legal action against them. Oversight responsibility for the investment banks' part in these transactions lay with both the banks themselves and the federal regulators. Investment banks told us that they had vetted transactions involving Enron through their risk management and internal control systems. Since Enron's collapse, these firms have been reportedly taking some steps to strengthen their internal controls, in part because they are now more sensitive to reputation risk.

Federal financial regulators noted that before Enron's collapse they had not viewed structured transactions with investment-grade counterparties as particularly high risk in their exams. Subsequently, they are refining their approach to supervising structured transactions, and bank regulators now plan to include more transactions in their exams. Regulators are currently conducting targeted reviews of structured finance transactions at large firms, and plan to develop guidance or best practices that clarify their expectations for sound control and oversight mechanisms.

In the wake of the scandals, research analysts at investment banks who made favorable recommendations for failed firms have also come under public scrutiny. Investment banks allegedly pressured analysts covering Enron and Global Crossing to give investors favorable or misleading investment recommendations in order to keep or win lucrative work from the companies, creating serious conflicts of interest.

Although the investment banks denied the allegations, several have been investigated by regulators and involved in litigation about conflicts of interest between their research and investment banking departments. Certain federal regulators and self-regulatory organizations have all adopted additional regulations addressing such conflicts. Although investment banks are not typically responsible for their client's accounting, it is a violation of law to facilitate transactions that an investment bank knows will materially misstate the client's financial statements.

Since investment banks may be tempted to participate in profitable but questionable transactions, it is especially important that regulators be alert to this and be ready to use their enforcement tools to deter such action. GAO was encouraged that investment banks and regulators are strengthening their oversight of the appropriateness of transactions, but it is too soon to evaluate the effectiveness of reforms. This report focuses primarily on five structured finance transactions involving Enron and investment banks for the period 1992 through 2001.

No publicly available documents on or references to investment banks' involvement in designing or implementing structured transactions used by Global Crossing were found. The report addresses other client relationships that investment banks had with Global Crossing, primarily through their research analysts. Through the transactions we describe in this report, investment banks facilitated complex structured finance transactions, despite allegedly knowing that Enron would use deceptive accounting and tax strategies. Complaints filed by the Securities and Exchange Commission (SEC) and individual investors also allege that, through various transactions, Enron and its officers and directors engaged in a scheme to defraud investors by inappropriately reporting the transactions in Enron's financial statements, and consequently misrepresenting Enron's true financial condition.

Section 705 GASP

This section analyzes and reports on the role of Investment Banks with respect to the corporate scandals conducted by Enron and WorldCom executives.

As a result, management needs to incorporate careful consideration and appropriate review of:

- off-balance sheet transactions (refer to Section 402 of SOXBoK)
- avoiding conflicts of interest situations with Investment Bankers
- issuance of Misleading Stock Reports by Research Analyst

Investment Bankers need to be aware that in some cases courts have found that an investment banker owes a fiduciary duty to a company if the investment banker evaluated and considered the appropriateness of unsuccessful financial transactions that caused the company's bankruptcy. Investment bankers are often retained to advise on a course of action that a board of directors has already determined to pursue. The banker's role in helping the board achieve those objectives is set forth in an agreement known as an engagement letter, and the banker's duties to the client are limited to the terms of that letter. Moreover, the advice that investment banks provide is largely subjective.

Special Purpose Entities (SPE)

Management needs to incorporate accounting and financial disclosure requirements when using SPEs to raise capital. The duties of the investment bankers in such transactions depend on the role the investment bankers played. If the SPE issues securities through a public offering that it sells to investors in order to raise capital, and the investment bank acquires the securities from the SPE with the intent to subsequently distribute them, then the investment bank is acting as an underwriter. As an underwriter, the investment banker would have duties of due diligence and disclosure.

Ownership interests in an entity, including an SPE, are considered financial assets. When assets of this type are sold or transferred to another entity, Financial Accounting Standards (FAS) 140, *Accounting for Transfers and Servicing of Financial Assets and Extinguishments of Liabilities*, provides the accounting guidance related to the transaction.

CHAPTER 8:
Corporate and Criminal Fraud Accountability

Practitioners Perspective and Regulation Synopsis

It is against the law to retaliate or take retribution of any kind against an employee providing an indication of illegal activities within a company. The reporting employee has every right to civil action against the company – also without repercussion – if any retribution or discrimination is imposed.

Regulation Text

SEC. 801. SHORT TITLE.
This title may be cited as the "Corporate and Criminal Fraud Accountability Act of 2002".

SEC. 802. CRIMINAL PENALTIES FOR ALTERING DOCUMENTS.
(a) IN GENERAL.—Chapter 73 of title 18, United States Code, is amended by adding at the end the following:

§ 1519. Destruction, alteration, or falsification of records in Federal investigations and bankruptcy

Whoever knowingly alters, destroys, mutilates, conceals, covers up, falsifies, or makes a false entry in any record, document, or tangible object with the intent to impede, obstruct, or influence the investigation or proper administration of any matter within the jurisdiction of any department or agency of the United States or any case filed under title 11, or in relation to or contemplation of any such matter or case, shall be fined under this title, imprisoned not more than 20 years, or both.

§ 1520. Destruction of corporate audit records

(a)(1) Any accountant who conducts an audit of an issuer of securities to which section 10A(a) of the Securities Exchange Act of 1934 (15 U.S.C. 78j–1(a)) applies, shall maintain all audit or review workpapers for a period of 5 years from the end of the fiscal period in which the audit or review was concluded.

(2) The Securities and Exchange Commission shall promulgate, within 180 days, after adequate notice and an opportunity for comment, such rules and regulations, as are reasonably necessary, relating to the retention of relevant records such as workpapers, documents that form the basis of an audit or review, memoranda, correspondence, communications, other documents, and records (including electronic records) which are created, sent, or received in connection with an audit or review and contain conclusions, opinions, analyses, or financial data relating to such an audit or review, which is conducted by any accountant who conducts an audit of an issuer of securities to which section 10A(a) of the Securities Exchange Act of 1934 (15 U.S.C. 78j–1(a)) applies. The Commission may, from time to time, amend or supplement the rules and regulations that it is required to promulgate under this section, after adequate notice and an opportunity for comment, in order to ensure that such rules and regulations adequately comport with the purposes of this section.

(b) Whoever knowingly and willfully violates subsection (a)(1), or any rule or regulation promulgated by the Securities and Exchange Commission under subsection (a)(2), shall be fined under this title, imprisoned not more than 10 years, or both.

(c) Nothing in this section shall be deemed to diminish or relieve any person of any other duty or obligation imposed by Federal or State law or regulation to maintain, or refrain from destroying, any document."

(b) CLERICAL AMENDMENT.—The table of sections at the beginning of chapter 73 of title 18, United States Code, is amended by adding at the end the following new items:
1519. Destruction, alteration, or falsification of records in Federal investigations and bankruptcy.
1520. Destruction of corporate audit records."

SEC. 803. DEBTS NONDISCHARGEABLE IF INCURRED IN VIOLATION OF SECURITIES FRAUD LAWS.

Section 523(a) of title 11, United States Code, is amended—

(1) in paragraph (17), by striking "or" after the semicolon;

(2) in paragraph (18), by striking the period at the end and inserting "; or"; and

(3) by adding at the end, the following:

(19) that—

(A) is for—

(i) the violation of any of the Federal securities laws (as that term is defined in section 3(a)(47) of the Securities Exchange Act of 1934), any of the State securities laws, or any regulation or order issued under such Federal or State securities laws; or

(ii) common law fraud, deceit, or manipulation in connection with the purchase or sale of any security; and

(B) results from—

(i) any judgment, order, consent order, or decree entered in any Federal or State judicial or administrative proceeding;

(ii) any settlement agreement entered into by the debtor; or

(iii) any court or administrative order for any damages, fine, penalty, citation, restitutionary payment, disgorgement payment, attorney fee, cost, or other payment owed by the debtor.".

SEC. 804. STATUTE OF LIMITATIONS FOR SECURITIES FRAUD.

(a) IN GENERAL.—Section 1658 of title 28, United States Code, is amended—

(1) by inserting "(a)" before "Except"; and

(2) by adding at the end the following:

(b) Notwithstanding subsection (a), a private right of action that involves a claim of fraud, deceit, manipulation, or contrivance in contravention of a regulatory requirement concerning the securities laws, as defined in section 3(a)(47) of the Securities Exchange Act of 1934 (15 U.S.C. 78c(a)(47)), may be brought not later than the earlier of—

(1) 2 years after the discovery of the facts constituting the violation; or

(2) 5 years after such violation."

(b) EFFECTIVE DATE.—The limitations period provided by section 1658(b) of title 28, United States Code, as added by this section, shall apply to all proceedings addressed by this section that are commenced on or after the date of enactment of this Act.

(c) NO CREATION OF ACTIONS.—Nothing in this section shall create a new, private right of action.

SEC. 805. REVIEW OF FEDERAL SENTENCING GUIDELINES FOR OBSTRUCTION OF JUSTICE AND EXTENSIVE CRIMINAL FRAUD.
(a) ENHANCEMENT OF FRAUD AND OBSTRUCTION OF JUSTICE SENTENCES.—Pursuant to section 994 of title 28, United States Code, and in accordance with this section, the United States Sentencing Commission shall review and amend, as appropriate, the Federal Sentencing Guidelines and related policy statements to ensure that—
   (1) the base offense level and existing enhancements contained in United States Sentencing Guideline 2J1.2 relating to obstruction of justice are sufficient to deter and punish that activity;
   (2) the enhancements and specific offense characteristics relating to obstruction of justice are adequate in cases where—
      (A) the destruction, alteration, or fabrication of evidence involves—
         (i) a large amount of evidence, a large number of participants, or is otherwise extensive;
         (ii) the selection of evidence that is particularly probative or essential to the investigation; or
         (iii) more than minimal planning; or
      (B) the offense involved abuse of a special skill or a position of trust;
   (3) the guideline offense levels and enhancements for violations of section 1519 or 1520 of title 18, United States Code, as added by this title, are sufficient to deter and punish that activity;
   (4) a specific offense characteristic enhancing sentencing is provided under United States Sentencing Guideline 2B1.1 (as in effect on the date of enactment of this Act) for a fraud offense that endangers the solvency or financial security of a substantial number of victims; and
   (5) the guidelines that apply to organizations in United States Sentencing Guidelines, chapter 8, are sufficient to deter and punish organizational criminal misconduct.

(b) EMERGENCY AUTHORITY AND DEADLINE FOR COMMISSION ACTION.—The United States Sentencing Commission is requested to promulgate the guidelines or amendments provided for under this section as soon as practicable, and in any event not later than 180 days after the date of enactment of this Act, in accordance with the procedures set forth in section 219(a) of the Sentencing Reform Act of 1987, as though the authority under that Act had not expired.

SEC. 806. PROTECTION FOR EMPLOYEES OF PUBLICLY TRADED COMPANIES WHO PROVIDE EVIDENCE OF FRAUD.
(a) IN GENERAL.—Chapter 73 of title 18, United States Code, is amended by inserting after section 1514 the following:

§ 1514A. Civil action to protect against retaliation in fraud cases
(a) WHISTLEBLOWER PROTECTION FOR EMPLOYEES OF PUBLICLY TRADED COMPANIES.—No company with a class of securities registered under section 12 of the Securities Exchange Act of 1934 (15 U.S.C. 78l), or that is required to file reports under section 15(d) of the Securities Exchange Act of 1934 (15 U.S.C. 78o(d)), or any officer, employee, contractor, subcontractor, or agent of such company, may discharge, demote, suspend, threaten, harass, or in any other manner discriminate against an employee in the terms and conditions of employment because of any lawful act done by the employee—
  (1) to provide information, cause information to be provided, or otherwise assist in an investigation regarding any conduct which the employee reasonably believes constitutes a violation of section 1341, 1343, 1344, or 1348, any rule or regulation of the Securities and Exchange Commission, or any provision of Federal law relating to fraud against shareholders, when the information or assistance is provided to or the investigation is conducted by—
    (A) a Federal regulatory or law enforcement agency;
    (B) any Member of Congress or any committee of Congress; or
    (C) a person with supervisory authority over the employee (or such other person working for the employer who has the authority to investigate, discover, or terminate misconduct); or

(2) to file, cause to be filed, testify, participate in, or otherwise assist in a proceeding filed or about to be filed (with any knowledge of the employer) relating to an alleged violation of section 1341, 1343, 1344, or 1348, any rule or regulation of the Securities and Exchange Commission, or any provision of Federal law relating to fraud against shareholders.

(b) ENFORCEMENT ACTION.—
 (1) IN GENERAL.—A person who alleges discharge or other discrimination by any person in violation of subsection (a) may seek relief under subsection (c), by—
  (A) filing a complaint with the Secretary of Labor; or
  (B) if the Secretary has not issued a final decision within 180 days of the filing of the complaint and there is no showing that such delay is due to the bad faith of the claimant, ringing an action at law or equity for de novo review in the appropriate district court of the United States, which shall have jurisdiction over such an action without regard to the amount in controversy.
 (2) PROCEDURE.—
  (A) IN GENERAL.—An action under paragraph (1)(A) shall be governed under the rules and procedures set forth in section 42121(b) of title 49, United States Code.
  (B) EXCEPTION.—Notification made under section 42121(b)(1) of title 49, United States Code, shall be made to the person named in the complaint and to the employer.
  (C) BURDENS OF PROOF.—An action brought under paragraph (1)(B) shall be governed by the legal burdens of proof set forth in section 42121(b) of title 49, United States Code.
  (D) STATUTE OF LIMITATIONS.—An action under paragraph (1) shall be commenced not later than 90 days after the date on which the violation occurs.

(c) REMEDIES.—
 (1) IN GENERAL.—An employee prevailing in any action under subsection (b)(1) shall be entitled to all relief necessary to make the employee whole.
 (2) COMPENSATORY DAMAGES.—Relief for any action under paragraph (1) shall include—

(A) reinstatement with the same seniority status that the employee would have had, but for the discrimination;
(B) the amount of back pay, with interest; and
(C) compensation for any special damages sustained as a result of the discrimination, including litigation costs, expert witness fees, and reasonable attorney fees.

(d) RIGHTS RETAINED BY EMPLOYEE.—Nothing in this section shall be deemed to diminish the rights, privileges, or remedies of any employee under any Federal or State law, or under any collective bargaining agreement."

(b) CLERICAL AMENDMENT.—The table of sections at the beginning of chapter 73 of title 18, United States Code, is amended by inserting after the item relating to section 1514 the following new item:
"1514A. Civil action to protect against retaliation in fraud cases."

SEC. 807. CRIMINAL PENALTIES FOR DEFRAUDING SHAREHOLDERS OF PUBLICLY TRADED COMPANIES.

(a) IN GENERAL.—Chapter 63 of title 18, United States Code, is amended by adding at the end the following:

§ 1348. Securities fraud

Whoever knowingly executes, or attempts to execute, a scheme or artifice—
(1) to defraud any person in connection with any security of an issuer with a class of securities registered under section 12 of the Securities Exchange Act of 1934 (15 U.S.C. 78l) or that is required to file reports under section 15(d) of the Securities Exchange Act of 1934 (15 U.S.C. 78o(d)); or
(2) to obtain, by means of false or fraudulent pretenses, representations, or promises, any money or property in connection with the purchase or sale of any security of an issuer with a class of securities registered under section 12 of the Securities Exchange Act of 1934 (15 U.S.C. 78l) or that is required to file reports under section 15(d) of the Securities Exchange Act of 1934 (15 U.S.C. 78o(d)); shall be fined under this title, or imprisoned not more than 25 years, or both."

(b) CLERICAL AMENDMENT.—The table of sections at the beginning of chapter 63 of title 18, United States Code, is amended by adding at the end the following new item:
"1348. Securities fraud."

Section 801 – Short Title
Domain: Not Applicable
Knowledge Area: Not Applicable
SOX Process: Not Applicable

Section 801 Synopsis
May also be referenced as: Corporate and Criminal Fraud Accountability Act of 2002

Section 801 GASP
Not Applicable.

Section 802 – Criminal Penalties for Altering Documents
Domain: Deterrence, Governance
Knowledge Area: Law, Ethics and Compliance, Internal and External Audit
SOX Process: Audit Compliance and Enforcement

Section 802 Synopsis
This section establishes criminal penalties of a fine and/or imprisonment of up to 20 years for:
- changing or destroying documents in the course of an investigation with the intent of changing the outcome of the investigation
- destruction of evidence that supports the audit process (ie the shredding of documents by Arthur Anderson employees prior to the investigation during the Enron proceedings)

This section also establishes criminal penalties of a fine and/or imprisonment of up to 10 years for willfully neglecting to keep audit paperwork and supporting documents for a minimum of five years.

Section 802 GASP

- retain all supporting evidence for any audit of financial statements that are register with the SEC for a minimum of five years; save manual work papers and evidence that supports audit conclusions, including documents, memoranda, correspondence such as email, and electronic records
- designate an employee to maintain audit documentation in an orderly fashion, so that any audit professional without prior knowledge of the company or the audit conducted should be able to review the documents and come up with the same audit conclusion
- the company should establish a firm 'records management and retention policy' that is communicated to all employees regarding the retention of documents, including electronic correspondence

Section 803 – Debts Non-dischargeable if incurred in Violation of Securities Fraud Laws

Domain: Responsibility
Knowledge Area: Law, Ethics and Compliance
SOX Process: Audit Compliance and Enforcement

Section 803 Synopsis

Section 523(a) of Title 11, United States Code is amended to add that any and all debts incurred as a result of criminal activity against federal or state security laws will not be discharged. Examples of these obligations are:

- settlements
- attorney fees
- court costs
- any other debt incurred as a result of a violation

Section 803 GASP

Not Applicable.

Section 804 – Statute of Limitations for Securities Fraud
Domain: Governance
Knowledge Area: Law, Ethics and Compliance
SOX Process: Audit Compliance and Enforcement

Section 804 Synopsis
The securities fraud statute is amended, so that a claim alleging fraud can be filed 'not later than the earlier of ... '
- two years of discovering the facts of the violation
- within five years after the violation
- if a fraudulent act is not discovered within five years of occurrence, it cannot be prosecuted under this section
- if it were discovered within four years, you would now have one year remaining to file a claim
- if discovered within one year of the violation, you would have two years to file a claim

Section 804 GASP
The 'whistleblower' should be aware that there is a statute of limitations within which securities fraud can be reported. A claim must be brought to the SEC, as defined in the Securities Exchange Act of 1934, no later than:
- two years after discovering the facts of the violation, or five years after the violation occurred

A training program, administered through the human resources department, ensures all employees are aware of the details of the 'whistleblower' program, and should include the statue of limitations for reporting violations.

Section 805 – Review of Federal Sentencing Guidelines for Obstruction of Justice and Extensive Criminal Fraud
Domain: Responsibility, Governance
Knowledge Area: Law, Ethics and Compliance
SOX Process: Audit Compliance and Enforcement

Section 805 Synopsis
This section orders the United States Sentencing Commission to revisit and update the sentences for the following specific offenses committed under the SOX Act:

- excessive destruction of probative documents
- abuse of special skills or a position of trust
- minimal planning
- the results are financial insolvency of a large number of victims

Section 805 GASP
Corporate council should review the sentencing guidelines and inform executive management, Board of Directors, Audit Committee and employees throughout the organization of the responsibilities and penalties related to criminal fraud.

Section 806 – Protection for Employees of Publicly Traded Companies Who Provide Evidence of Fraud
Domain: Responsibility, Transparency
Knowledge Area: Law, Ethics and Compliance, Information Technology
SOX Process: Audit Compliance and Enforcement

Section 806 Synopsis
- Often referred to as the 'whistleblower protection' section of the SOX Act, it requires that whistleblowers (employees providing evidence or notification of possible fraud) be protected from retaliatory action on the part of the company or any of its employees.
- The company must take steps to protect the anonymity of the informant and protect him/her against retaliation. Relief (civil remedy) under the law is available for employees who experience reprisal, including wrongful discharge or less drastic acts of discrimination, such as demotion or poor performance reviews.
- Whistleblower program details must be communicated to all employees. Note: SOX does not include a punitive or exemplary damages provision, nor does it allow for a recovery of a percentage of the fraud.

Section 806 GASP
- Best practice in this area is to establish a toll-free phone number for anonymously reporting suspected infractions or fraudulent business activities. If it is not feasible for a company to maintain their own toll-free number, then an outsourced service contracted by the reporting entity's human resources department should be established. In addition, someone must be appointed to address and resolve all reported infractions, while

insuring that individual remains anonymous during the initial disclosure process. Creation of a communication plan and internal training program ensures that all levels of employees are aware of what constitutes a violation and explains their rights and responsibilities in case of an infraction.
- It is typical for a corporation to outsource the whistleblower services to a provider that specializes in receiving anonymous submissions across categories, not limited to accounting and auditing related complaints. The service provider typically honors the wishes of the submitter regarding personally identifiable information along with the complaint. The handling and resolution of accounting and auditing related complaints is typically done by the internal audit department and/or the audit committee.
- All employees must be trained and given access to this service, whether it is via a readily accessible online or telephone interface. Training includes an understanding of what constitutes a violation of the whistleblower protection, and employee rights, urgency in reporting potential violations, and responsibilities in the event of such a violation. This training may take the form of inclusion in the employee handbook and/or separate notification via company newsletter or memo.
- The jurisdiction of legal enforcement of whistleblower protection lies within the context of the US Department of Labor(DOL), and therefore is limited to the DOL's jurisdiction.

Section 807 – Criminal Penalties for Defrauding Shareholders of Publicly Traded Companies

Domain: Responsibility, Governance
Knowledge Area: Law, Ethics and Compliance
SOX Process: Audit Compliance and Enforcement

Section 807 Synopsis

A fine and/or imprisonment of not more than 25 years will be imposed upon any person who:
- knowingly uses a false representation of a security to defraud someone else
- deliberately misrepresents the value of a publicly traded security in exchange for an investment of money or property

Section 807 GASP

Corporate council should review the sentencing guidelines and inform executive management, board of directors, audit committee and employees throughout the organization, of the responsibilities and penalties related to criminal fraud.

CHAPTER 9:
White-Collar Crime Penalty Enhancements

Practitioners Perspective and Regulation Synopsis

Title IX creates significant expansion of the penalties associated with white collar crime. These additions were considered necessary in order to provide greater deterrence and punishment in support of the existing law. The Sarbanes-Oxley Act of 2002 demanded that criminal penalties be significantly enhanced for any person(s) who attempts or conspires to commit any offense within the following previously issued legislation:

- The United States Code covering Mail and Wire Fraud
- Employee Retirement Income Security Act of 1974
- The United States Sentencing Commission
- The Security Exchange Act of 1934

Most importantly, previous legislation covering white collar crime now includes significant penalties associated with failure of corporate officers to certify that the company's financial condition and results of operations are materially and fairly represented.

Regulation Text

SEC. 901. SHORT TITLE.
This title may be cited as the "White-Collar Crime Penalty Enhancement Act of 2002".

H. R. 3763—61

SEC. 902. ATTEMPTS AND CONSPIRACIES TO COMMIT CRIMINAL FRAUD OFFENSES.

(a) IN GENERAL.—Chapter 63 of title 18, United States Code, is amended by inserting after section 1348 as added by this Act the following:

"§ 1349. Attempt and conspiracy

"Any person who attempts or conspires to commit any offense under this chapter shall be subject to the same penalties as those prescribed for the offense, the commission of which was the object of the attempt or conspiracy.

(b) CLERICAL AMENDMENT.—The table of sections at the beginning of chapter 63 of title 18, United States Code, is amended by adding at the end the following new item: "1349. Attempt and conspiracy.".

SEC. 903. CRIMINAL PENALTIES FOR MAIL AND WIRE FRAUD.

(a) MAIL FRAUD.—Section 1341 of title 18, United States Code, is amended by striking "five" and inserting "20".

(b) WIRE FRAUD.—Section 1343 of title 18, United States Code, is amended by striking "five" and inserting "20".

SEC. 904. CRIMINAL PENALTIES FOR VIOLATIONS OF THE EMPLOYEE RETIREMENT INCOME SECURITY ACT OF 1974.

Section 501 of the Employee Retirement Income Security Act of 1974 (29 U.S.C. 1131) is amended—
(1) by striking "$5,000" and inserting "$100,000";
(2) by striking "one year" and inserting "10 years"; and
(3) by striking "$100,000" and inserting "$500,000".

SEC. 905. AMENDMENT TO SENTENCING GUIDELINES RELATING TO CERTAIN WHITE-COLLAR OFFENSES.

(a) DIRECTIVE TO THE UNITED STATES SENTENCING COMMISSION.— Pursuant to its authority under section 994(p) of title 18, United States Code, and in accordance with this section, the United States Sentencing Commission shall review and, as appropriate, amend the Federal Sentencing Guidelines and related policy statements to implement the provisions of this Act.

(b) REQUIREMENTS.—In carrying out this section, the Sentencing Commission shall—
- (1) ensure that the sentencing guidelines and policy statements reflect the serious nature of the offenses and the penalties set forth in this Act, the growing incidence of serious fraud offenses which are identified above, and the need to modify the sentencing guidelines and policy statements to deter, prevent, and punish such offenses;
- (2) consider the extent to which the guidelines and policy statements adequately address whether the guideline offense levels and enhancements for violations of the sections amended by this Act are sufficient to deter and punish such offenses, and specifically, are adequate in view of the statutory increases in penalties contained in this Act;
- (3) assure reasonable consistency with other relevant directives and sentencing guidelines;
- (4) account for any additional aggravating or mitigating circumstances that might justify exceptions to the generally applicable sentencing ranges; H. R. 3763—62
- (5) make any necessary conforming changes to the sentencing guidelines; and
- (6) assure that the guidelines adequately meet the purposes of sentencing, as set forth in section 3553(a)(2) of title 18, United States Code.

(c) EMERGENCY AUTHORITY AND DEADLINE FOR COMMISSION ACTION.—The United States Sentencing Commission is requested to promulgate the guidelines or amendments provided for under this section as soon as practicable, and in any event not later than 180 days after the date of enactment of this Act, in accordance with the procedures set forth in section 219(a) of the Sentencing Reform Act of 1987, as though the authority under that Act had not expired.

SEC. 906. CORPORATE RESPONSIBILITY FOR FINANCIAL REPORTS.
(a) IN GENERAL.—Chapter 63 of title 18, United States Code, is amended by inserting after section 1349, as created by this Act, the following:

"§ 1350. Failure of corporate officers to certify financial reports
(a) CERTIFICATION OF PERIODIC FINANCIAL REPORTS.—Each periodic report containing financial statements filed by an issuer with the Securities Exchange Commission pursuant to section 13(a) or 15(d) of the Securities Exchange Act of 1934 (15 U.S.C. 78m(a) or 78o(d)) shall be accompanied by a written statement by the chief executive officer and chief financial officer (or equivalent thereof) of the issuer.

"(b) CONTENT.—The statement required under subsection (a) shall certify that the periodic report containing the financial statements fully complies with the requirements of section 13(a) or 15(d) of the Securities Exchange Act pf 1934 (15 U.S.C. 78m or 78o(d)) and that information contained in the periodic report fairly presents, in all material respects, the financial condition and results of operations of the issuer.

"(c) CRIMINAL PENALTIES.—Whoever—
(1) certifies any statement as set forth in subsections
(a) and (b) of this section knowing that the periodic report accompanying the statement does not comport with all the requirements set forth in this section shall be fined not more than $1,000,000 or imprisoned not more than 10 years, or both; or
"(2) willfully certifies any statement as set forth in subsections
(a) and (b) of this section knowing that the periodic report accompanying the statement does not comport with all the requirements set forth in this section shall be fined not more than $5,000,000, or imprisoned not more than 20 years, or both.".

(b) CLERICAL AMENDMENT.—The table of sections at the beginning of chapter 63 of title 18, United States Code, is amended by adding at the end the following:
"1350. Failure of corporate officers to certify financial reports."

Section 901 – Short Title
Domain: Not Applicable
Knowledge Area: Not Applicable
SOX Process: Not Applicable

Section 901 Synopsis
This may also be referred to as the 'White Collar Crime Penalty Enhancement Act of 2002'.

Section 901 GASP
Not Applicable.

Section 902 – Attempts and Conspiracies to Commit Criminal Fraud Offenses
Domain: Deterrence
Knowledge Area: Law, Ethics and Compliance
SOX Process: Audit Compliance and Enforcement

Section 902 Synopsis
Amends Title 18 of the United States Code, Crimes and Criminal Procedures for Mail Fraud, by adding to existing laws covering defrauding shareholders, to include anyone who attempts or conspires with someone to break the law is now subject to the same penalties as those who committed the criminal fraud offenses.

Section 902 GASP
Not Applicable.

Section 903 – Criminal Penalties for Mail and Wire Fraud
Domain: Deterrence
Knowledge Area: Law, Ethics and Compliance
SOX Process: Audit Compliance and Enforcement

Section 903 Synopsis
Amends Section 1341 of Title 18, United States Code, Crimes and Criminal Procedures for Mail and Wire Fraud, sets penalties for defrauding shareholders using the Postal Service, by changing the penalty to a maximum of 20 years imprisonment.

Section 903 GASP
Not Applicable.

Section 904 – Criminal Penalties for Violations of the Employee Retirement Income Security Act of 1974

Domain: Deterrence
Knowledge Area: Law, Ethics and Compliance
SOX Process: Audit Compliance and Enforcement

Section 904 Synopsis
Employee Retirement Security Act of 1974, and Title 29 of United States Code, Section 1131 covering Labor, are amended for penalties associated with a conviction to include:

- fined not more than $100,000
- maximum penalty for criminal violations of the Employee Retirement Income Security Act of 1974 (ERISA) from one year to ten years imprisonment
- the fine imposed upon an individual in violation shall not exceed $500,000

Section 904 GASP
Not Applicable.

Section 905 – Amendment to Sentencing Guidelines Relating to Certain White-Collar Offenses

Domain: Deterrence
Knowledge Area: Law, Ethics and Compliance
SOX Process: Audit Compliance and Enforcement

Section 905 Synopsis
Essentially this section gives authority under the law to enforce the provisions of the act for criminal penalties. It uses the authority established in the Sentencing Commission to provide guidance to the courts for determining a particular sentence to be imposed for the purpose of proposing a sufficient sentence, but not greater then necessary to comply with the purposes established under section 3553 (a) (2) of Title 18 of the United States Code.

Section 905 GASP
Not Applicable.

Section 906 – Corporate Responsibility for Financial Reports
Domain: Replacement, Transparency, Accountability
Knowledge Area: Law, Ethics and Compliance
SOX Process: Audit Compliance and Enforcement

Section 906 Synopsis
This section adds Section 1350 to Title 18 of the United States Code, which contains a certification requirement with specific federal criminal provisions, and that is separate and distinct from the certification requirement mandated by Section 302 of SOA 2002:

- **Certification of Periodic Financial Reports** - Each periodic report containing financial statements filed by an issuer with the Securities Exchange Commission pursuant to section 13(a) or 15(d) of the Securities Exchange Act of 1934 (15 U.S.C. 78m(a) or 78o(d)) shall be accompanied by a written statement by the chief executive officer and chief financial officer (or equivalent thereof) of the issuer.
- **Content** - The statement required under subsection (a) shall certify that the periodic report containing the financial statements fully complies with requirements of section 13(a) or 15(d) of the Securities Exchange Act pf (!1) 1934 (15 U.S.C. 78m or 78o(d)) and that information contained in the periodic report fairly presents, in all material respects, the financial condition and results of operations of the issuer.
- **Criminal Penalties** – Whoever; certifies any statement as set forth in subsections (a) and (b) of this section knowing that the periodic report accompanying the statement does not comport with all the requirements set forth in this section shall be fined not more than $1,000,000 or imprisoned not more than 10 years, or both; or
- Willfully certifies any statement as set forth in subsections (a) and (b) of this section knowing that the periodic report accompanying the statement does not comport with all the requirements set forth in this section shall be fined not more than $5,000,000, or imprisoned not more than 20 years, or both.

Section 906 GASP

- Best Practice is ensuring that the Chief Executive Officer (CEO) and Chief Financial Officer (CFO) are made fully aware of their responsibilities for issuing a written statement certifying that the periodic reports containing the financial statements fully comply with the requirements of the SEC Act of 1934, and that information contained in the periodic report fairly represents, in all material aspects, the financial condition and results of operations of the issuer.
- A review of internal accounting policies in relation to requirements noted in the SEC Act of 1934 is also essential to ensure compliance with the act.
- Executive officers at corporate headquarters and all subsidiary business units understand their responsibility for establishing an effective level of internal control and their certification of financial reports is based on their ability to detect and prevent significant aspects of fraud in their organization.

CHAPTER 10:
Corporate Tax Returns

Practitioners Perspective and Regulation Synopsis

Title X establishes who is authorized to sign a corporation's Federal income tax return.

Regulation Text

**SEC. 1001. SENSE OF THE SENATE REGARDING THE SIGNING OF CORPORATE
TAX RETURNS BY CHIEF EXECUTIVE OFFICERS.**

It is the sense of the Senate that the Federal income tax return of a corporation should be signed by the chief executive officer of such corporation.

Section 1001 – Sense of the Senate Regarding the Signing of Corporate Tax Returns by Chief Executive Officers

Domain:	Accountability; Responsibility
Knowledge Area:	Law, Ethics and Compliance
SOX Process:	Audit Compliance and Enforcement

Section 1001 Synopsis

This is a change from previous legislation, which allowed CFO or controller to sign the Tax return. With Title X, the intent is similar to other areas of SOX and provides for the CEO to be individually accountable and responsible for reporting results. SOX ties this into corporate tax returns the same way that Titles III and IV make CEOs responsible for financial reporting.

IT may have a role by maintaining the data that is reviewed by auditors and signed off by CEOs.

Section 1001 GASP

The Chief Executive Officer (CEO) should sign the corporation's Federal income tax return.

CHAPTER 11:
Corporate Fraud Accountability

Practitioners Perspective and Regulation Synopsis
Title XI amends the Unites States Code and Securities Exchange Act of 1934, setting penalties, rules and guidelines surrounding corporate fraud, including:
- penalties for anyone tampering with evidence or impeding an official proceeding
- penalties for anyone retaliating against individuals who report Federal offenses
- maximum fine and imprisonment penalties
- temporary orders requiring issuers to escrow extraordinary payments during the course of investigations
- prohibition of individuals who have violated sections of the Securities Exchange Act from serving as officers or directors
- responsibilities of the United States Sentencing Commission regarding securities and accounting fraud

Regulation Text

SEC. 1101. SHORT TITLE.
This title may be cited as the "Corporate Fraud Accountability Act of 2002".

SEC. 1102. TAMPERING WITH A RECORD OR OTHERWISE IMPEDING AN OFFICIAL PROCEEDING.
Section 1512 of title 18, United States Code, is amended—
    (1) by redesignating subsections (c) through (i) as subsections (d) through (j), respectively; and

(2) by inserting after subsection (b) the following new subsection:
"(c) Whoever corruptly—
"(1) alters, destroys, mutilates, or conceals a record, document, or other object, or attempts to do so, with the intent to impair the object's integrity or availability for use in an official proceeding; or
"(2) otherwise obstructs, influences, or impedes any official proceeding, or attempts to do so, shall be fined under this title or imprisoned not more than 20 years, or both."

SEC. 1103. TEMPORARY FREEZE AUTHORITY FOR THE SECURITIES EXCHANGE COMMISSION.

(a) IN GENERAL.—Section 21C(c) of the Securities Exchange Act of 1934 (15 U.S.C. 78u–3(c)) is amended by adding at the end the following:
"(3) TEMPORARY FREEZE.—
"(A) IN GENERAL.—
"(i) ISSUANCE OF TEMPORARY ORDER.— Whenever, during the course of a lawful investigation involving possible violations of the Federal securities laws by an issuer of publicly traded securities or any of its directors, officers, partners, controlling persons, agents, or employees, it shall appear to the Commission that it is likely that the issuer will make extraordinary payments (whether compensation or otherwise) to any of the foregoing persons, the Commission may petition a Federal district court for a temporary order requiring the issuer to escrow, subject to court supervision, those payments in an interest-bearing account for 45 days.
"(ii) STANDARD.—A temporary order shall be entered under clause (i), only after notice and opportunity for a hearing, unless the court determines that notice and hearing prior to entry of the order would be impracticable or contrary to the public interest.
"(iii) EFFECTIVE PERIOD.—A temporary order issued under clause (i) shall—
"(I) become effective immediately;
"(II) be served upon the parties subject to it; and
"(III) unless set aside, limited or suspended by a court of competent jurisdiction, shall remain effective and enforceable for 45 days.

"(iv) EXTENSIONS AUTHORIZED.—The effective period of an order under this subparagraph may be extended by the court upon good cause shown for not longer than 45 additional days, provided that the combined period of the order shall not exceed 90 days.

"(B) PROCESS ON DETERMINATION OF VIOLATIONS.—

"(i) VIOLATIONS CHARGED.—If the issuer or other person described in subparagraph (A) is charged with any violation of the Federal securities laws before the expiration of the effective period of a temporary order under subparagraph (A) (including any applicable extension period), the order shall remain in effect, subject to court approval, until the conclusion of any legal proceedings related thereto, and the affected issuer or other person, shall have the right to petition the court for review of the order.

"(ii) VIOLATIONS NOT CHARGED.—If the issuer or other person described in subparagraph (A) is not charged with any violation of the Federal securities laws before the expiration of the effective period of a temporary order under subparagraph (A) (including any applicable extension period), the escrow shall terminate at the expiration of the 45-day effective period (or the expiration of any extension period, as applicable), and the disputed payments (with accrued interest) shall be returned to the issuer or other affected person."

(b) TECHNICAL AMENDMENT.—Section 21C(c)(2) of the Securities Exchange Act of 1934 (15 U.S.C. 78u–3(c)(2)) is amended by striking "This" and inserting "paragraph (1)".

SEC. 1104. AMENDMENT TO THE FEDERAL SENTENCING GUIDELINES.

(a) REQUEST FOR IMMEDIATE CONSIDERATION BY THE UNITED STATES SENTENCING COMMISSION.—Pursuant to its authority under section 994(p) of title 28, United States Code, and in accordance with this section, the United States Sentencing Commission is requested to—

(1) promptly review the sentencing guidelines applicable to securities and accounting fraud and related offenses;

(2) expeditiously consider the promulgation of new sentencing guidelines or amendments to existing sentencing guidelines to provide an

enhancement for officers or directors of publicly traded corporations who commit fraud and related offenses; and

(3) submit to Congress an explanation of actions taken by the Sentencing Commission pursuant to paragraph (2) and Commission may have for combating offenses described in paragraph (1).

(b) CONSIDERATIONS IN REVIEW.—In carrying out this section, the Sentencing Commission is requested to—

(1) ensure that the sentencing guidelines and policy statements reflect the serious nature of securities, pension, and accounting fraud and the need for aggressive and appropriate law enforcement action to prevent such offenses;

(2) assure reasonable consistency with other relevant directives and with other guidelines;

(3) account for any aggravating or mitigating circumstances that might justify exceptions, including circumstances for which the sentencing guidelines currently provide sentencing enhancements;

(4) ensure that guideline offense levels and enhancements for an obstruction of justice offense are adequate in cases where documents or other physical evidence are actually destroyed or fabricated;

(5) ensure that the guideline offense levels and enhancements under United States Sentencing Guideline 2B1.1 (as in effect on the date of enactment of this Act) are sufficient for a fraud offense when the number of victims adversely involved is significantly greater than 50;

(6) make any necessary conforming changes to the sentencing guidelines; and

(7) assure that the guidelines adequately meet the purposes of sentencing as set forth in section 3553 (a)(2) of title 18, United States Code.

(c) EMERGENCY AUTHORITY AND DEADLINE FOR COMMISSION ACTION.—The United States Sentencing Commission is requested to promulgate the guidelines or amendments provided for under this section as soon as practicable, and in any event not later than the 180 days after the date of enactment of this Act, in accordance with the procedures sent forth in section 21(a) of the Sentencing Reform Act of 1987, as though the authority under that Act had not expired.

SEC. 1105. AUTHORITY OF THE COMMISSION TO PROHIBIT PERSONS FROM SERVING AS OFFICERS OR DIRECTORS.

(a) SECURITIES EXCHANGE ACT OF 1934.—Section 21C of the Securities Exchange Act of 1934 (15 U.S.C. 78u–3) is amended by adding at the end the following:

"(f) AUTHORITY OF THE COMMISSION TO PROHIBIT PERSONS FROM SERVING AS OFFICERS OR DIRECTORS.—In any cease-and-desist proceeding under subsection (a), the Commission may issue an order to prohibit, conditionally or unconditionally, and permanently or for such period of time as it shall determine, any person who has violated section 10(b) or the rules or regulations thereunder, from acting as an officer or director of any issuer that has a class of securities registered pursuant to section 12, or that is required to file reports pursuant to section 15(d), if the conduct of that person demonstrates unfitness to serve as an officer or director of any such issuer.".

(b) SECURITIES ACT OF 1933.—Section 8A of the Securities Act of 1933 (15 U.S.C. 77h–1) is amended by adding at the end of the following:

"(f) AUTHORITY OF THE COMMISSION TO PROHIBIT PERSONS FROM SERVING AS OFFICERS OR DIRECTORS.—In any cease-and-desist proceeding under subsection (a), the Commission may issue an order to prohibit, conditionally or unconditionally, and permanently or for such period of time as it shall determine, any person who has violated section 17(a)(1) or the rules or regulations thereunder, from acting as an officer or director of any issuer that has a class of securities registered pursuant to section 12 of the Securities Exchange Act of 1934, or that is required to file reports pursuant to section 15(d) of that Act, if the conduct of that person demonstrates unfitness to serve as an officer or director of any such issuer.".

SEC. 1106. INCREASED CRIMINAL PENALTIES UNDER SECURITIES EXCHANGE ACT OF 1934.

Section 32(a) of the Securities Exchange Act of 1934 (15 U.S.C. 78ff(a)) is amended—

(1) by striking "$1,000,000, or imprisoned not more than 10 years" and inserting "$5,000,000, or imprisoned not more than 20 years"; and

(2) by striking "$2,500,000" and inserting "$25,000,000".

SEC. 1107. RETALIATION AGAINST INFORMANTS.

(a) IN GENERAL.—Section 1513 of title 18, United States Code, is amended by adding at the end the following:

"(e) Whoever knowingly, with the intent to retaliate, takes any action harmful to any person, including interference with the lawful employment or livelihood of any person, for providing to a law enforcement officer any truthful information relating to the commission or possible commission of any Federal offense, shall be fined under this title or imprisoned not more than 10 years, or both.".

Section 1101 – Short Title
SOXBoK Domain: Not Applicable
Knowledge Area: Not Applicable
SOX Process: Not Applicable

Section 1101 Synopsis
Corporate Fraud and Accountability Act of 2002.

Section 1101 GASP
Not Applicable.

Section 1102 – Tampering with a Record or Otherwise Impeding an Official Proceeding
Domain: Accountability; Responsibility; Governance
Knowledge Area: Law, Ethics and Compliance; Information Technology
SOX Process: Audit Compliance and Enforcement

Section 1102 Synopsis
Any attempt (successful or not) to tamper with evidence and/or documents in an official proceeding will be punished by up to 20 years imprisonment and/or fines.

Section 1102 GASP
The company should ensure that it has an updated records retention policy that covers electronic and paper-based records. The policy should articulate steps followed in the event of a litigation hold. The policy should also indicate the consequences of tampering with evidence/documents in an official proceeding.

The company should appoint someone who will be responsible for maintaining a document retention system, which includes:
- safeguards against tampering
- retrieval system, whereby documents can be made readily available to Federal Officials
- document destruction policies, as determined necessary by corporate legal council

Corporate counsel, upon notification of an investigation, takes action to secure all evidence and documents that might be used in that investigation. Activities to include:
- gathering all evidence and documents used in the proceedings
- retrieving back-up tapes or drives from their normal rotation and storing them separately
- inventory keeping of all documents used
- securing documents in a safe location

Section 1103 – Temporary Freeze Authority for the Securities and Exchange Commission

Domain: Accountability
Knowledge Area: Law, Ethics and Compliance
SOX Process: Audit Compliance and Enforcement

Section 1103 Synopsis

- During a lawful investigation of an SEC cease-and-desist proceeding, if the issuing company is likely to be required to make extraordinary payments -- whether compensation or otherwise -- to any of the foregoing persons, the SEC can petition the Federal district court to issue a temporary order requiring the issuer to escrow those payments. The escrow can extend no less than 45 and no more than 90 days after notice and opportunity for a hearing.
- The term extraordinary payment is defined by the court during the course of an investigation. However, in general terms, it is any payment that would not be considered ordinary, typical, normal, planned, or expected during the course of normal business.

- If violations are charged, the order remains in effect until the legal proceedings conclude. If violations are not charged, the payments kept in escrow are returned to the issuer. The escrow can extend no less than 45 and no more than 90 days after notice and opportunity for a hearing.

Section 1103 GASP
- Best practice is to begin making payments to an escrow account if it appears that the company will owe money as a result of an investigation or court proceeding. If it is ruled that the company must pay the fee, it will already be held in escrow. If it is decided that the company is not liable, the funds will be returned.

Section 1104 – Amendment to the Federal Sentencing Guidelines
Domain: Accountability; Governance
Knowledge Area: Law, Ethics and Compliance
SOX Process: Audit Compliance and Enforcement

Section 1104 Synopsis
- This section lists responsibilities of the United States Sentencing Commission, the body that publishes the sentencing guidelines used by all United States courts and the probation system.
- The US Sentencing Commission should promptly review current sentencing guidelines 'applicable to securities and accounting fraud and related offenses.' During this review, they must ensure that sentencing policies and guidelines are aggressive, appropriate, consistent, and adequate.
- Any actions taken as a result of their review of sentencing policies must be justified and published no more than 180 days from the enactment of the Sarbanes-Oxley Act of 2002.

Section 1104 GASP
- These actions have been completed by the US Sentencing Commission. (See the US Sentencing Commission.) The final report is available to the public.
- Corporate counsel should understand and make management aware of sentencing policies and guidelines.

Section 1105 – Authority of the Commission to Prohibit Persons from Serving as Officers or Directors

Domain: Responsibility
Knowledge Area: Law, Ethics and Compliance
SOX Process: Audit Compliance and Enforcement

Section 1105 Synopsis

During a cease-and-desist proceeding, the Securities Exchange Commission can prohibit an individual who has violated sections 10(b) or 17(a)(1) of the Securities Exchange Act of 1934 from serving as an officer or director of an issuing company.

- Securities Exchange Act of 1934, section 10(b) prohibits fraud, manipulation and insider trading when buying/selling securities or executing a security-based swap agreement.
- Security Exchange Act of 1934, section 17(a)(1) requires SEC brokers and dealers to create, disseminate, and retain reports according to Securities Exchange Commission mandate.

Section 1105 GASP

- Human resources should conduct a detailed background check on any potential directors or officers, to verify they have not been convicted or investigated for violating SEC rules, or federal or statutory laws; based on the reports, decide whether the candidates are suitable for hiring. The company should consider using a background check service.

Section 1106 – Increased Criminal Penalties under Securities Exchange Act of 1934

Domain: Deterrence
Knowledge Area: Law, Ethics and Compliance
SOX Process: Audit Compliance and Enforcement

Section 1106 Synopsis

- The maximum penalty fine for an individual, as defined by the SEC, has been increased from $1,000,000 to $5,000,000, and the maximum prison sentence has been increased from 10 years to 20 years. The maximum penalty fine for someone other than an individual (ie a corporation or legal entity) has increased from $2,500,000 to $25,000,000.

Section 1106 GASP

- Officers and directors should build their awareness about the enhanced penalties.
- Corporate counsel should disseminate information to the board members that penalties for violating the Security Exchange Act have been doubled for individual offenders, and increased ten-fold for companies or corporations if convicted.

Section 1107 – Retaliation Against Informants

Domain: Deterrence
Knowledge Area: Law, Ethics and Compliance
SOX Process: Audit Compliance and Enforcement

Section 1107 Synopsis

- Any person who retaliates or discriminates against another for providing truthful information to the SEC regarding a Federal offense will be fined or imprisoned for up to 10 years, or both.

Section 1107 GASP

- Allow a fair investigation or court proceeding to take place. Be co-operative and refrain from interacting with other witnesses.
- Officers and directors should build their awareness of the penalties for retaliation or discrimination related to this section and disseminate to appropriate management.

References

Contributors: Jeanette M. Franzel, John J. Reilly, Jr., William E. Boutboul, Cheryl E. Clark, Robert W. Gramling, Wilfred B. Holloway, Michael C. Hrapsky, Catherine M. Hurley, Charles E. Norfleet, Judy K. Pagano, Sidney H. Schwartz, Jason O. Strange, Patricia A. Summers, and Walter K. Vance (2003). *PUBLIC ACCOUNTING FIRMS Required Study on the Potential Effects of Mandatory Audit Firm Rotation.* Retrieved August 3, 2007, from the United States General Accounting Office website: http://www.gao.gov/new.items/d04216.pdf

The Securities and Exchange Commission (2003). 17 CFR PARTS 210, 240, 249 and 274 [RELEASE NO. 33-8183; 34-47265; 35-27642; IC-25915; IA-2103, FR-68, File No. S7-49-02] RIN 3235-AI73 Strengthening the Commission's Requirements Regarding Auditor Independence. Retrieved August 6, 2007, from the Securities and Exchange Commission website: http://www.sec.gov/rules/final/33-8183.htm

Office of the Law Revision Council (2007), *Search the United States Code.* Retrieved May 3, 2007, from US House of Representatives web site: http://uscode.house.gov/search/criteria.shtml

U.S. Securities and Exchange Commission (2007), *Securities Exchange Act of 1934,* Retrived May 3, 2007, from U.S. Securities and Exchange Commission web site: http://www.sec.gov/divisions/corpfin/34act/index1934.shtml
Clement, Paul D., Prezioso, Giovanni P., Humes, Richard M., Hardy, Melinda, Karr, Thomas J. (2005) , *No. 04-1723 In the Supreme Court of the United States HENRY C. YUEN, ET AL., PETITIONERS v. SECURITIES AND*

EXCHANGE COMMISSION, ET AL. On Petition for a Writ of Certiorari to the United States Court of Appeals for the Ninth Circuit Brief for the Federal Respondent In Opposition, Retrieved May 7, 2007, from United States Department of Justice web site: http://www.usdoj.gov/osg/briefs/2005/0responses/2004-1723.resp.html

Steer, John R. (2003), The Sentencing Commission's Implementation of the Sarbanes-Oxley Act, Retrieved May 3, 2007, from United States Sentencing Commission web site: http://www.ussc.gov/corp/Steer-PLI-2003.pdf

United States Securities and Exchange Commission: Form 20-F: website: www.sec.gov/about/forms/form20-f.pdf <http://www.sec.gov/about/forms/form20-f.pdf> .

United States Securities and Exchange Commission: Form 40-F: website: www.sec.gov/about/forms/form40-f.pdf <http://www.sec.gov/about/forms/form40-f.pdf> .

Glossary

Anti-trust	The general process of preventing monopoly practices or breaking up monopolies that restrict competition. The term anti-trust derives from the common use of the trust organizational structure in the late 1800s and early 1900s to monopolize markets.
Audit and attest services	Services provided for professional examination and verification of a company's accounting documents and supporting data for the purpose of rendering an opinion on the fairness with which they present, in all material respects, the financial position, results of operations, and its cash flows, and conformity with generally accepted accounting principles.
Audit Board	In the United States, the Auditing Standards Board (ASB) is the senior technical committee designated by the American Institute of Certified Public Accountants (AICPA) to issue auditing, attestation, and quality control statements, standards and guidance to certified public accountants (CPAs) for non-public company audits. Created in October 1978, it is composed of 19 members representing various industries and sectors, including public accountants and private, educational, and governmental entities. It issues pronouncements in the form of statements, interpretations, and guidelines, which all CPAs must adhere to when performing audits and attestations.
Audit Committee	Oversees the accounting and financial reporting processes of the issuer and oversees audits of the financial statements of the issuer. The committee is established by the board of directors of an issuer comprised of members of the board of directors of an issuer, or may be comprised of the entire board of directors.

Audit fee	Fee paid by a company to an audit accounting firm for the professional examination and verification of its accounting documents and supporting data.
Audit market	The organized exchange of audit and attest services between buyers and sellers within a specific geographic area and during a given period of time.
Auditor independence	The idea that the auditor of record is exclusively concerned with examination and verification of a company's accounting documents and supporting data without bias or conflicts of interest. Professional auditing standards require an auditor to be independent and avoid situations that may lead others to doubt its independence, referred to as being independent in fact as well as in appearance. Auditor independence is an important factor in establishing the credibility of the audit opinion.
Auditor, auditor of record, and registered public accounting firm	Generally refers to an independent public accounting firm registered with SEC that performs audits and reviews of public company financial statements and prepares attestation reports filed with SEC. In the future, these public accounting firms must be registered with Public Company Accounting Oversight Board (PCAOB) as required by the Sarbanes-Oxley Act of 2002.
Barriers to entry	Institutional, governmental, technological, or economic factors that limit the flow of new entrants into profitable markets. Possible barriers to entry may include resources, patents and copyrights or technical expertise, reputation, litigation and insurance risks, and start-up costs. Barriers to entry are a key reason for market power. In particular, monopoly and oligopoly often owe their market power to assorted barriers to entry.
Beneficial Owner	Issuing company directors, or officers. Individuals who directly or indirectly own more than 10% of any class of the issuing company's stock, security or equity.
Beneficiary	A person or entity named in a will or a financial contract as the inheritor of property when the property owner dies.
Benefit Pension Plan	A type of retirement plan, usually tax exempt, wherein an employer makes contributions toward a pool of funds set aside for an employee's future benefit. The pool of funds is then invested on the employee's behalf, allowing the employee to receive benefits upon retirement.

Blackout Period	1. This term is often in regards to contracts, policies and business activities. For example, when a political party is unable to advertise for a set amount of time before an election. 2. In a firm, a blackout period may happen because a plan is being restructured or altered, for example, if a pension fund is shifting from one fund manager to another at a different bank.
Board of Directors	Individuals elected by the shareholders of a corporation who carry out certain tasks established in the charter.
Bottom line loss	Occurs when gross sales minus taxes, interest, depreciation, and other expenses are negative. Also called negative net earnings, income, or profit.
CEO	Chief Executive Officer. The CEO is the highest ranking executive in a company, whose main responsibilities include developing and implementing high-level strategies, making major corporate decisions, managing the overall operations and resources of a company, and acting as the main point of communication between the board of directors and the corporate operations. The CEO will often have a position on the board, and in some cases is even the chair.
CFO	Chief Financial Officer. The CFO is the senior manager who is responsible for overseeing the financial activities of an entire company. This includes signing checks, monitoring cash flow, and financial planning.
COBIT	Control Objectives for Information and related Technology (COBIT). A set of best practices (framework) for information technology (IT) management created by the Information Systems Audit and Control Association (ISACA), and the IT Governance Institute (ITGI) in 1992. COBIT provides managers, auditors, and IT users with a set of generally accepted measures, indicators, processes and best practices to assist them in maximizing the benefits derived through the use of information technology and developing appropriate IT governance and control in a company.
Code of Ethics	Standards to promote honest and ethical conduct, including the ethical handling of actual or apparent conflicts of interest between personal and professional relationships.

Commission – Securities and Exchange Commission (SEC)	The SEC is a government commission created by Congress to regulate the securities markets and protect investors. In addition to regulation and protection, it also monitors the corporate takeovers in the US. The SEC is composed of five commissioners appointed by the US President and approved by the Senate. The statutes administered by the SEC are designed to promote full public disclosure and to protect the investing public against fraudulent and manipulative practices in the securities markets. Generally, most issues of securities offered in interstate commerce, through the mail or on the internet, must be registered with the SEC.
Commission Description	The members of the Board shall take such action (including hiring of staff, proposal of rules, and adoption of initial and transitional auditing and other professional standards) as may be necessary or appropriate to enable the Commission to determine, not later than 270 days after the date of enactment of this Act, that the Board is so organized and has the capacity to carry out the requirements of this title, and to enforce compliance with this title by registered public accounting firms, and associated persons thereof. The Commission shall be responsible, prior to the appointment of the Board, for the planning, establishment, and administrative transition to the Board's operation. Source: SOX Act, 2002.
Competition	In general, the actions of two or more rivals in pursuit of the same objective. In the context of markets, the specific objective is selling or buying goods. Competition tends to come in two varieties – competition among the few, which is a market with a small number of sellers (or buyers), such that each seller (or buyer) has some degree of market control, and competition among the many, which is a market with so many buyers and sellers that none is able to influence the market price or quantity exchanged.
Concentration ratio	The proportion of total output in an industry that is produced by a given number of the largest firms in the industry. The two most common concentration ratios are for the four largest firms and the eight largest firms. The four-firm concentration ratio is the proportion of total output produced by the four largest firms in the industry and the eight-firm concentration ratio is the proportion of total output produced by the eight largest firms in the industry.
Corporation Counsel	The title given to the chief legal officer in a company, who handles legal claims against the company, including negotiating settlements and defending the company when it is sued.

COSO	COSO [Committee of Sponsoring Organizations] is a voluntary private sector organization dedicated to improving the quality of financial reporting through business ethics, effective internal controls, and corporate governance.
Disclosure control	Procedures designed by a company to ensure that information required for disclosure can be accumulated and communicated to company's management, including the CEO and CFO, in a timely manner in order to allow sufficient time for decision-making. Disclosure controls should effectively record, process, summarize and report needed disclosures within the time periods specified by the Commission for reporting required disclosures.
Disgorgement	The forced giving up of profits obtained by illegal or unethical acts. A court may order wrongdoers to pay back illegal profits, with interest, to prevent unjust enrichment. Disgorgement is a remedy and not a punishment.
Disgorgement Fund	A fund used to hold money that was repaid or taken back from a defendant as a result of being found guilty of violating the laws set forth in the Securities Act of 1934, and to be used for the relief of victims.
Due diligence	The process of investigation performed by investors, accountants and other market participants into the details of a potential investment, such as an examination of operations and management and the verification of material facts. Obtaining a comment letter written by independent accountants to an underwriter is part of that underwriter's due diligence.
Economies of scale	Declining long-run average costs that occur as a firm increases all inputs and expands its scale of production, realized through operational efficiencies. Economies of scale can be accomplished because as production increases, the cost of producing each additional unit falls.
Economies of scope	Declining long-run average costs that occur due to changes in the mix of output between two or more products. This refers to the potential cost savings from joint production – even if the products are not directly related to each other. Economies of scope are also said to exist if it is less costly for one firm to produce two separate products than for two specialized firms to produce them separately.
Electronic Gathering, Analysis and Retrieval system (EDGAR)	The electronic filing system created by the Securities and Exchange Commission for the purpose of increasing efficiency and accessibility to corporate filings. This system is used by all publicly traded companies when submitting required documents to the SEC. Corporate documents are time sensitive, and the creation of EDGAR has greatly decreased the time it takes for corporate documents to become publicly available.

Employee Retirement Income Security Act (ERISA) of 1974	The Employee Retirement Income Security Act of 1974 (ERISA) protects the retirement assets of Americans, by implementing rules that qualified plans must follow to ensure that plan fiduciaries do not misuse plan assets.
Equity security:	The common stock of a corporation. The ownership interest of a shareholder in a company.
Extraordinary Payment	The term has not been explicitly defined, but in situations such as the Gemstar case, the 'SEC appears to be taking an aggressive position on the scope of the definition of "extraordinary payments.' (http://www.nixonpeabody.com/publications_detail3.asp?Type=P&PAID=&ID=370)
Fair Value Accounting	In accounting, fair value is used as an estimate of the market value of an asset (or liability) for which a market price cannot be determined (usually because there is no established market for the asset).
Federal antitrust laws	A series of federal laws intended to maintain competition and prevent businesses from getting a monopoly or unfairly obtaining or exerting market power. The first of these, the Sherman Antitrust Act, was passed in 1890. Two additional laws, the Clayton Act and the Federal Trade Commission Act, were enacted in 1914. These laws impose restrictions on business ownership, control, mergers, pricing, and how businesses go about competing (or co-operating) with each other.
Financial Expert	A person who has established a base of knowledge, through education and experience as a public accountant or auditor or a principal financial officer, comptroller, or principal accounting officer of an issuer, or from a position involving the performance of similar functions – included in the base of knowledge: (1) an understanding of generally accepted accounting principles and financial statements (2) experience in: (a) the preparation or auditing of financial statements of generally comparable issuers (b) the application of such principles in connection with the accounting for estimates, accruals, and reserves (3) experience with internal accounting controls (4) an understanding of audit committee functions
Generally Accepted Accounting Principles (GAAP)	The common set of accounting principles, standards and procedures that companies use to compile their financial statements. GAAP is a combination of authoritative standards (set by policy boards) and simply the commonly accepted ways of recording and reporting accounting information.

Going-concern opinion	Opinion that expresses substantial doubt about whether or not a company will continue to operate for 1 year beyond the financial statement date or go out of business and liquidate its assets. Indicated when there are substantial doubts about whether the company will be able to generate and/or raise enough resources to stay operational.
Gramm-Leach-Bliley Act	The Gramm-Leach-Bliley Act, also known as the Gramm-Leach-Bliley Financial Services Modernization Act, Pub. L. No. 106-102, 113 Stat. 1338 (November 12, 1999), is an Act of the United States Congress which repealed the Glass-Steagall Act, opening up competition among banks, securities companies and insurance companies. The Glass-Steagall Act prohibited a bank from offering investment, commercial banking, and insurance services. The Gramm-Leach-Bliley Act (GLBA) allowed commercial and investment banks to consolidate.
Hirschman-Herfindahl Index (HHI)	A measure of concentration of the production in an industry that is calculated as the sum of the squares of market shares for each firm. This is an alternative method of summarizing the degree to which an industry is oligopolistic and the relative concentration of market power held by the largest firms in the industry. The HHI gives a better indication of the relative market power of the largest firms than can be found with the four-firm and eight-firm concentration ratios.
Industry	A collection of firms that produce similar products sold in the same market. The concept of industry is most often used synonymously with market in most microeconomic analysis.
Insider	Issuing company directors, officers, or anyone with access to material information about the company before it becomes public knowledge.
Internal Controls	Internal control is broadly defined as a process, affected by an entity's board of directors, management, and other personnel, designed to provide reasonable assurance regarding the achievement of objectives including: effectiveness and efficiency of operations, reliability of financial reporting and compliance with applicable laws and regulations.
Investment Company Act of 1940	The **Investment Company Act of 1940** is an act of Congress. It was passed as a United States Public Law and is codified at 15 U.S.C. § 80a-1 through 15 U.S.C. § 80a-52.

Issuer	(a) Any entity who issues or proposes to issue any security, the securities of which are registered with the SEC by a member, broker or dealer, allowing them to effect any security transaction on a national securities exchange. (b) The person or persons performing the acts and assuming the duties of depositor or manager pursuant to the provisions of the trust or other agreement or instrument under which such securities are issued, the securities of which are registered with the SEC by a member, broker or dealer, allowing them to effect any security transaction on a national securities exchange.
Issuer (Issuing Company)	A legal entity that develops, registers, and sells securities for the purpose of financing its operations.
Loss Leader	The term loss leader implies that the firms bid unrealistically low fees ('low-balling') to obtain a new client. Once the new client is secured, the low audit fee, which alone may not be adequate to cover the cost of an audit and provide the firm with a reasonable margin, is offset by additional fees generated from other services, such as management consulting and tax.
Market	The organized exchange of commodities (goods, services, or resources) between buyers and sellers within a specific geographic area, and during a given period of time.
Market power	The power to profitably maintain prices above competitive levels for a significant amount of time. More generally, if it is the ability of sellers to exert influence over the price or quantity of a good, service, or commodity exchanged in a market. Market power depends on the number of competitors.
Market structure	The manner, in which a market is organized, based largely on the number of firms in the industry. The four basic market structure models are perfect competition, monopoly, monopolistic competition, and oligopoly. The primary difference between each is the number of firms on the supply side of a market. Both perfect competition and monopolistic competition have a large number of relatively small firms selling output. Oligopoly has a small number of relatively large firms. Monopoly has a single firm.

Materiality	If omission or misstatement of information could influence the decisions of users, then it would be considered material. Auditor should use the same materiality considerations in an audit of internal control over financial reporting, as would be used in planning the audit of the companies' financial statements. Materiality in an audit of internal control over financial reporting should be applied at both the financial statement level and individual account balance level. Materiality at the individual account balance level is necessarily lower then at the financial statement level.
Natural Person	A real human being, as distinguished from a corporation, which is often treated at law as a fictitious person.
Peer review	A part of the accounting profession's former self-regulatory system whereby accounting firms reviewed other firm's quality control systems for compliance with standards and membership requirements. The Sarbanes-Oxley Act of 2002 significantly overhauled the oversight and regulation of the accounting profession. Among other things, it established the Public Company Accounting Oversight Board to oversee the audit of public companies, including registering public accounting firms, establishing standards, and conducting compliance inspections, investigations, and disciplinary proceedings.
Penny Stock	A stock that trades at a relatively low price and market capitalization, usually outside of the major market exchanges. These types of stocks are generally considered to be highly speculative and high risk because of the lack of liquidity, large bid-ask spreads, small capitalization, and limited following and disclosure. They will often trade over the counter through the Over-The-Counter Bulletin Board (OTCBB) and pink sheets. **Author's Notes:** The term itself is a misnomer because there is no generally accepted definition of a penny stock. Some consider it to be any stock that trades for pennies or those that trade for under $5, while others consider any stock trading off of the major market exchanges as a penny stock. However, confusion can occur as there are some very large companies, based on market capitalization, that trade below $5 per share, while there are many very small companies that trade for $5 or more. The typical penny stock is a very small company with highly illiquid and speculative shares. The company will also generally be subject to limited listing requirements along with fewer filing and regulatory standards.

Predatory pricing	The process in which a firm with market power reduces prices below average total cost with the goal of forcing competitors into bankruptcy. This practice is most commonly undertaken by oligopolistic firms seeking to expand their market shares and gain greater market control. Anti-trust laws have outlawed predatory pricing, but this practice can be difficult to prove.
Principles-Based Accounting	Provides for few exact rules and little implementation guidance. Instead, general principles are put forward and companies must ensure that their financial statements fairly and accurately represent these principles. It can be considered that this type of system does not allow for less than ethical financial engineering, where complex transactions are undertaken in order to get around following specific rules-based accounting standards. It can also be considered, that a principles-based system allows too much leeway for companies, because they generally do not have to follow specific rules, only wide-arching principles.
Pro-Forma Figures	Pro Forma is a Latin term meaning 'for the sake of form'. In the investing world, it describes a method of calculating financial results in order to emphasize either current or projected figures.
Publicly listed companies (public companies)	A company which has issued securities (through an offering) that are traded on the open market. Used synonymously with public company. For the purposes of this report public companies include companies listed on the New York Stock Exchange, American Stock Exchange, and NASDAQ or traded on other over-the-counter markets such as Pink Sheets.
Retained earnings	Earnings not paid out as dividends but instead reinvested in the core business or used to pay off debt. Also called earned surplus, accumulated earnings, or unappropriated profit.
Rules-Based Accounting	Specific accounting rules are set forth and must be followed in order to comply with GAAP. For example, if a company leases capital equipment, the company must follow specific GAAP rules to determine if the transaction is an operating lease or a capital lease. The main difference being that a capital lease would have to appear on the balance sheet of the company. Therefore, two virtually identical lease transactions could be classified entirely differently based upon how they follow the GAAP leasing rules. Rules-based accounting standards, which are characterized by bright-line tests, multiple exceptions, a high level of detail, and internal inconsistencies.
Securities Exchange Act of 1934	The Securities Exchange Act of 1934 was created to provide governance of securities transactions on the secondary market (after issue) and regulate the exchanges and broker-dealers in order to protect the investing public.

Special Purpose Entity (SPE)	An SPE is a legal entity created by another entity (a sponsor) to carry out a specified purpose or activity, such as to consummate a specific transaction or series of transactions with a narrowly defined purpose.
Swap Agreement	'For purposes of subsection (a)(6), the term 'swap agreement' means any individually negotiated contract, agreement, warrant, note, or option that is based, in whole or in part, on the value of, any interest in, or any quantitative measure or the occurrence of any event relating to, one or more commodities, securities, currencies, interest or other rates, indices, or other assets, but does not include any other identified banking product, as defined in paragraphs (1) through (5) of subsection (a).' (GLB Act section 206(b))
Tight oligopoly	An oligopolistic market structure where the four firms hold over 60 per cent of the market. A loose oligopoly is a market structure with 8-15 firms and a four-firm concentration ratio below 40 per cent.
United States Code	The United States Code (U.S.C.) is a compilation and codification of the general and permanent federal law of the United States.
United States Sentencing Commission	The United States Sentencing Commission is an independent agency of the Judicial Branch of the United States Government and is responsible for the sentencing policy of the United States Federal Courts. The Commission promulgates the Federal Sentencing Guidelines, which replaced the prior system of indeterminate sentencing that allowed trial judges to give sentences ranging from probation to the maximum statutory punishment for the offense.
White Collar Crime	A crime committed by a person of respectability and high social status in the course of his occupation (Edwin Sutherland).
Working capital	Current assets minus current liabilities. Working capital measures how much in liquid assets a company has available to build its business. The number can be positive or negative, depending on how much debt the company is carrying. In general, companies that have a lot of working capital will be more successful since they can expand and improve their operations.

Abbreviations

AICPA	American Institute of Certified Public Accountants
ASB	Auditing Standards Board
CEO	Chief Executive Officer
CFO	Chief Financial Officer
CIO	Chief Information Officer
CoBiT	Control Objectives for Information and related Technology
COSO	Committee of Sponsoring Organizations (*of the Treadway Commission*)
CPA	Certified Public Accountants
CRM	Customer Relationship Management
EDGAR	Electronic Gathering, Analysis and Retrieval system
ERISA	Employee Retirement Income Security Act
ERP	Enterprise Resource Planning
FAS	Financial Accounting Standards
GAAP	Generally Accepted Accounting Principles
GASP	Generally Accepted SOX Principles (*sometimes Generally Accepted SOX Practices*)
GOA	(*United States*) General Accounting Office
GRC	Governance, Risk (*Management*), Compliance
HHI	Hirschman-Herfindahl Index
ICOFR	Internal Control over Financial Reporting
ISACA	Information Systems Audit and Control Association
ITGC	IT General Control
ITGI	IT Governance Institute
ITIL	IT Infrastructure Library
NASD	National Association of Securities Dealers

NASDAQ	National Association of Securities Dealers Automated
OTCBB	Over-The-Counter Bulletin Board
PCAOB	Public Company Accounting Oversight Board
R&CM	Risk and Control Matrix
SEC	Securities and Exchange Commission
SOA	Sarbanes-Oxley Act
SOD	Segregation of Duties
SOX	Interpretation of the Sarbanes-Oxley Act of 2002
SOX Act	Sarbanes-Oxley Act
SOXBoK	Sarbanes-Oxley Body of Knowledge
SPE	Special Purpose Entity(*ies*)
USC	United States Code

Appendix A: Mapping of Significant Accounts

Basic Financial Statement

Balance Sheet:

	Amount From Consolidated Financials	Analysis		Degree of Estimation (H=High, M=Moderate, L=Low)	Significant? Yes/No	Rationale for Conclusion	CORE BUSINESS PROCESSES	
		% of Assets	% of Equity					
Cash	$15,028,055	0.37%	1.08%	L				Process 1
Accounts Receivable	446,115,063	10.98%	31.93%	M				
Allowance for Bad Debts	(2,620,175)	-0.06%	-0.19%	H				
Inventories:	-							Process 2
Raw Material	422,530,453	10.40%	30.24%	L				
WIP and Finished Goods	585,152,914	14.40%	41.88%	M				
Lower Cost/Mkt. Adjustment	(21,504,148)	-0.53%	-1.54%	H				Process 3
Inventory Supplies	804,375	0.02%	0.06%	L				
Prepaid - Other	19,103,001	0.47%	1.37%	M				
Deferred Tax - Current	28,530,296	0.70%	2.04%	H				Process 4
Restricted Cash (collateralizing letters of credit)	36,056,229	0.89%	2.58%	L				
Total Current Assets	**1,529,196,064**	37.64%	109.45%					Process 5
Property, Plant and Equipment, net	1,406,986,721	34.63%	100.70%	L				
Accumulated Depreciation	(96,323,777)	-2.37%	-6.89%	M				
Intangible Assets, net	16,691,461	0.41%	1.19%	M				

Appendix A

Basic Financial Statement	Amount From Consolidated Financials	Analysis		Degree of Estimation (H=High, M=Moderate, L=Low)	Significant? Yes/No	Rationale for Conclusion	Process 1	Process 2	Process 3	Process 4	Process 5
Goodwill	1,186,635,399	29.21%	84.93%	H							
Other Assets	19,505,840	0.48%	1.40%	M							
Total Assets	**$4,062,691,708**	**100.00%**	**290.78%**								
Accounts Payable	$271,599,174	6.69%	19.44%	M							
Accrued Liabilities:	-										
Payroll and Employee Benefits	91,449,747	2.25%	6.55%	M							
Personal Property Taxes	39,433,628	0.97%	2.82%	M							
Environmental Claims	16,675,241	0.41%	1.19%	H							
Income Tax Payable	56,763,351	1.40%	4.06%	H							
Miscellaneous - Other Accruals	107,206,229	2.64%	7.67%	M							
Total Current Liabilities	**583,127,370**	**14.35%**	**41.74%**								
Revolving Credit Facility	153,992,773	3.79%	11.02%	L							
Senior Secured Notes	623,851,103	15.36%	44.65%	L							
Post-Retirement Health Benefits (excluding current portion)	945,611,249	23.28%	67.68%	M							
Pension Benefits (excluding current portion)	144,496,255	3.56%	10.34%	M							

Basic Financial Statement	Amount From Consolidated Financials	Analysis	Degree of Estimation (H=High, M=Moderate, L=Low)	Significant? Yes/No	Rationale for Conclusion
Other Liabilities:					
Environmental Costs - Long-term	60,535,454	1.49%	H		
Deferred Compensation	32,588,110	0.80%	M		
Deferred Tax - Non-current	75,659,888	1.86%	H		
Miscellaneous - Other liabilities	45,678,315	1.12%	M		
Total Liabilities	$2,665,540,518	65.61%			
Preferred Stock	$32,752	0.00%	L		
Common stock	24,954	0.00%	L		
Additional paid-in capital	1,144,159,736	28.16%	M		
Retained earnings	93,608,633	2.30%	M		
Dividends declared YTD	(34,792,176)	-0.86%	L		
Accumulated other comprehensive income	194,117,291	4.78%	H		
Total Stockholders Equity	$1,397,151,191	34.39%			
	$4,062,691,708	PROOF			

				Process 1
				Process 2
				Process 3
				Process 4
				Process 5

Appendix B: Entity Level Controls

Basic Financial Statement

Income Statement:	Amount From Consolidated Financials	Analysis		Degree of Estimation (H=High, M=Moderate, L=Low)	Significant? Yes/No	Rationale for Conclusion	CORE BUSINESS PROCESSES				
		% of Total Revenues	% of Equity				Process 1	Process 2	Process 3	Process 4	Process 5
SALES	0										
Product Sales, net	$2,173,548,544	97.68%	155.57%								
Freight	51,649,913	2.32%	3.70%								
Net Sales	**2,225,198,457**	**100.00%**	**159.27%**								
OPERATING COSTS AND EXPENSES	-										
Cost of Goods Sold:											
Product Costs	1,918,628,657	86.22%	137.32%								
Prepaid Customer Freight	51,649,913	2.32%	3.70%								
Property Tax / Insurance	18,740,720	0.84%	1.34%								
Miscellaneous - Other Costs of Goods Sold	15,161,452	0.68%	1.09%								
Depreciation and Amortization	58,688,365	2.64%	4.20%								
Selling, General, and Administrative Expenses:	-										
General and Administrative Costs	22,361,253	1.00%	1.60%								
Bad Debt Expense	1,573,552	0.07%	0.11%								

Appendix B

Basic Financial Statement	Amount From Consolidated Financials	Analysis		Degree of Estimation (H=High, M=Moderate, L=Low)	Significant? Yes/No	Rationale for Conclusion	Process 1	Process 2	Process 3	Process 4	Process 5
Miscellaneous - Other SG&A Costs	24,543,053	1.10%	1.76%								
Total Operating Costs and Expenses	**2,111,346,966**	**94.88%**	**151.12%**								
Total Operating Income	**113,851,491**	**5.12%**	**8.15%**								
OTHER INCOME/(EXPENSE)	-										
Interest Expense	(27,189,625)	-1.22%	-1.95%						X		
Other Income, net	2,763,472	0.12%	0.20%								
Total Other Income/(Expense)	**(24,426,153)**	**-1.10%**	**-1.75%**								
Net Income Before Income Taxes and Cumulative Effect of Change in Accounting Principle	*89,425,338*	*4.02%*	*6.40%*							X	
Income Tax Expense	22,138,979	0.99%	1.58%								X
Net Income	***$67,286,359***	***3.02%***	***4.82%***								X

Appendix C: Flowchart: Procure to Pay Process

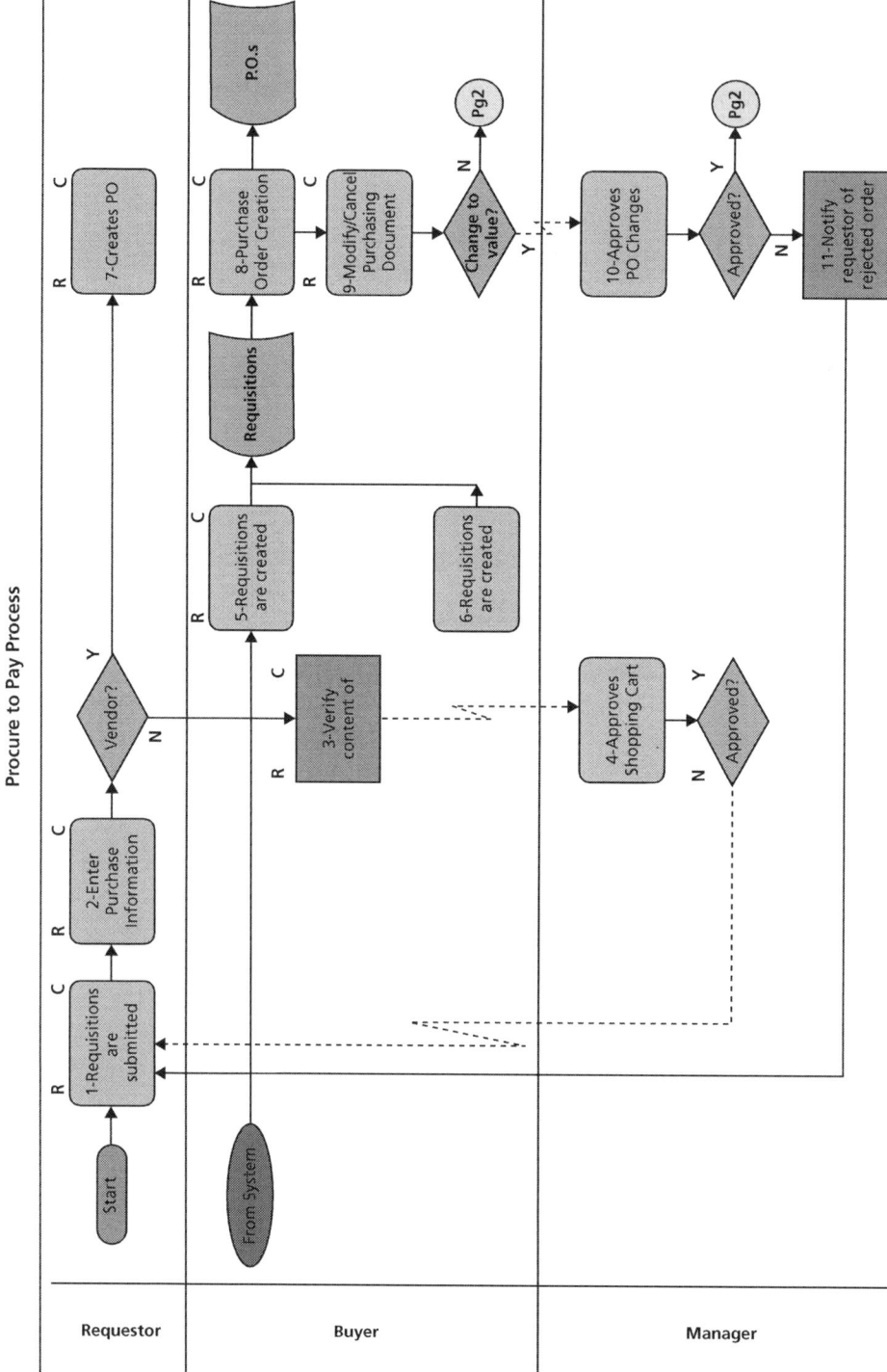

Appendix D: Procure to Pay

ACTIVITY SUMMARY		RISK SUMMARY							CONTROL SUMMARY					
Name of Activity	Description of Activity	Description of Risk	Risk Classification						Description of Control	Key Control	Type of control			Frequency of control
			PR	OR	SR	FR	VR	BR			S	O P	D	
1-Shopping carts are submitted	An end user completes a shopping cart in the system. System uses the default Cost Center assigned and looks up the defined approval levels. Based on these assignments, the systems sets up the work flow and forwards the shopping cart to the appropriate Manager(s) for approval.	Unauthorized or improper purchase requests are entered into the shopping cart and processed through the payables system.	X			X			Cost Center Assignments are defaulted in the Shopping Cart, and authorizations restrict user access to shopping carts for only those materials and items defined as attributes in the Organization Structure Table.		X	X		Event-Driven
1-Shopping carts are submitted	An end user completes a shopping cart in the system. System uses the default Cost Center assigned and looks up the defined approval levels. Based on these assignments, the systems sets up the work flow and forwards the shopping cart to the appropriate Manager(s) for approval.	Improper Account Number assignments could be entered and post through the system leading to mis-leading Financial Statements.				X			The G/L account validation table and accounting rules defined in the system ensures that a Balance Sheet Fixed Asset account is assigned for capital assets purchases. The GL account is validated against the cost center and business area defined within the validation tables.		X	X		Event-Driven

Step	Description	Risk			Control					Type
2-Enter Capital Purchase Information	Internal Orders that are entered for capital purchases, the system forces the Project ID to be entered using the the Material Group.	Capital Asset purchases are not classified or properly controlled.	X	X	The system sets up an additional approval level by checking the Project ID and starts the work flow for the shopping cart to be approved by the responsible manager.		X	X		Event-Driven
3-Verifies content of shopping cart	For Orders, the Buyer verifies the content of the shopping cart orders. The system uses workflow to route the shopping cart orders for approval. Clicking on the Approval Button routes the requisition to the next person defined within the Cost Center.	Unauthorized or unapproved requisitions could be processed by the Procurement department, resulting in higher costs, inadequate/Incorrect material ordered.	X	X	Only authorized purchasing personnel have system access rights to approve shopping carts.	Y		X	X	Event-Driven
3-Verifies content of shopping cart	For Orders, the Buyer verifies the content of the shopping cart orders. The system uses workflow to route the shopping cart orders for approval. Clicking on the Approval Button routes the requisition to the next person defined within the Cost Center.	Unauthorized or unapproved requisitions could be processed by the Procurement department, resulting in higher costs, inadequate/Incorrect material ordered.	X	X	Access to update the Approval and Organizational Structure Control tables is restricted. Changes to these tables require Ticket to be created and the reason for the change has to be properly documented.	Y		X	X	Event-Driven

Appendix E: Test Lead Sheet

TEST INFORMATION

Core Business Process:		Process Owner(s):
Sub-Process:		
Test Date:		Other Contacts:
Auditors/Testers:		
Corresponding Control Matrix:		

Control Objective:

Risk Description:

Overall Results:

Remediation Recommendations:

SCOPE OF TESTING AND SAMPLING PROCESS

Scope Statement:

TEST PROCEDURES & RESULTS

Test Procedures	Sample Size	Operationally Effective Yes = Pass No = Fail	Testing Worksheet	Test Results, Observations & Notes

Control Description:

TEST SIGN-OFF AND REVIEW

		TEST MATRIX ID:
Core Business Process:		o
Sub-Process:		
Corresponding Control Matrix:		
Key Control Numbers:		

Made in the USA
Columbia, SC
29 June 2019